CNC PROGRAMMING WORKBOOK

MILL

By Matthew Manton and Duane Weidinger

camInstructor

CNC Programming Workbook - Mill
Published by
CamInstructor Incorporated
330 Chandos Crt.
Kitchener, Ontario
N2A 3C2
www.caminstructor.com

Date: June 1, 2013
Author: Matthew Manton and Duane Weidinger
ISBN: 978-1-897466-84-1

National Library of Canada Cataloguing in Publication

To order additional copies of the book contact:
CamInstructor Inc.
330 Chandos Crt, Kitchener, ON, N2A 3C2
Phone 1-877-873-6867
Fax 1-866-741-8421
email sales@caminstructor.com

Printed in Canada

November 29, 2017

TABLE OF CONTENTS

TABLE OF CONTENTS

TABLE OF CONTENTS

CNC PROGRAMMING
WORKBOOK

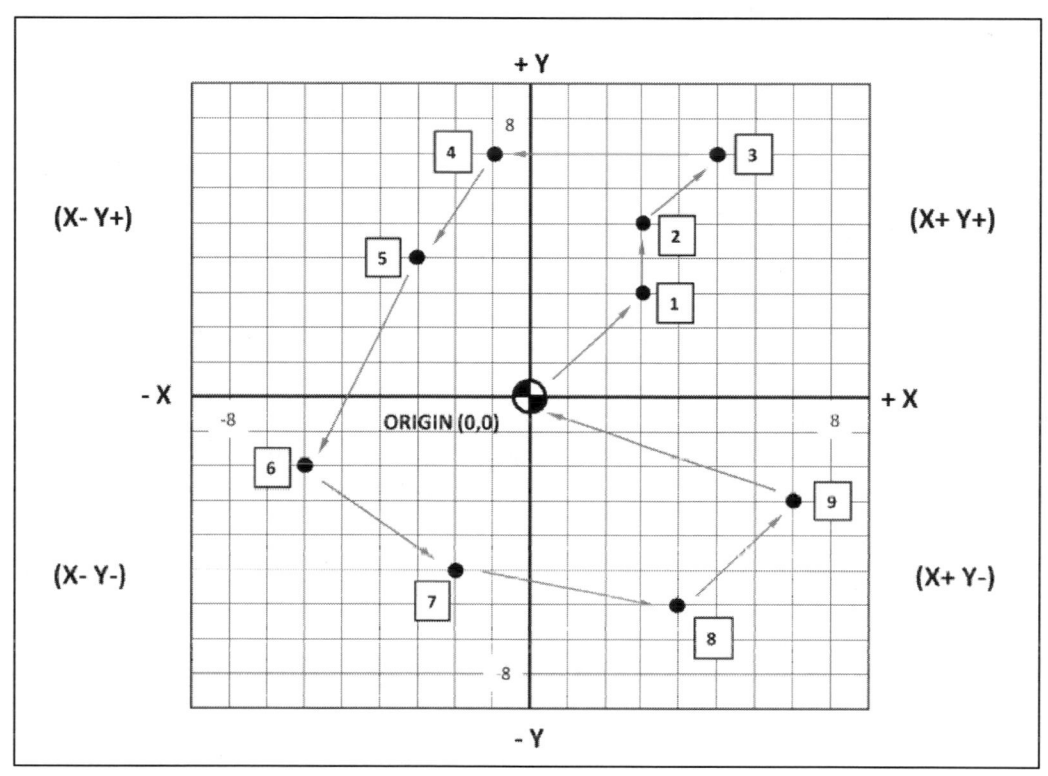

MILL-LESSON-1
ABSOLUTE & INCREMENTAL POSITIONING

camInstructor

Step 1 - Plug in your headphones or make sure your speakers are plugged in and turned on.

Step 2 – Log into the caminstructor site.

Step 3 - Click on Getting Started and watch the video through to the end. Feel free to pause and rewind the video if you need to watch something again.

Step 4 - Click on Lesson 1 and then click on Lesson-1 – Unit-1, as indicated it is 9 minutes long.

Step 5 - Proceed through the Videos in the proper order and make sure to follow along with the Workbook. Good luck and have fun.

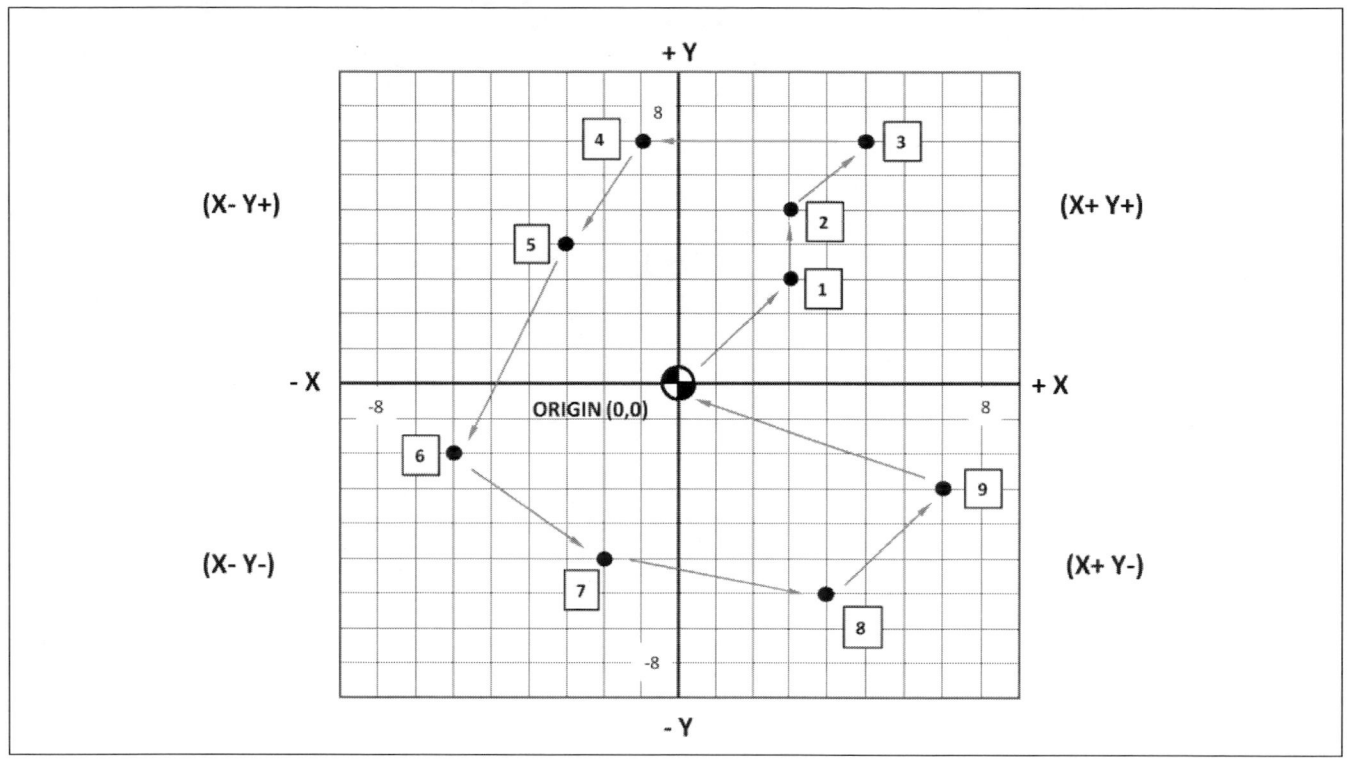

G90 ABSOLUTE PROGRAMMING

All axis motions are based on a fixed zero reference point, known as ABSOLUTE ZERO (part zero).
Each coordinate is in relation to this absolute zero using Cartesian Co-ordinates.

G91 INCREMENTAL PROGRAMMING

All axis motions are based on the distance to the next location.
Each coordinate is based on how far the cutter is to move from start to finish.

✎ *STARTING AT THE POINT O (ORIGIN), DESCRIBE THE PATH FROM O THROUGH ALL 9 POINTS AND BACK TO THE POINT O USING G90 & G91*

G90	X	Y	G91	X	Y
O (Origin)	0	0	O → 1	3	3
1	3	3	1 → 2	0	2
2	3	5	2 → 3	2	2
3	5	7	3 → 4	-6	0
4	-1	7	4 → 5	-2	-3
5	-3	4	5 → 6	-3	-6
6	-6	-2	6 → 7	4	-3
7	-2	-5	7 → 8	6	-1
8	4	-6	8 → 9	3	3
9	7	-3	9 → O	-7	3

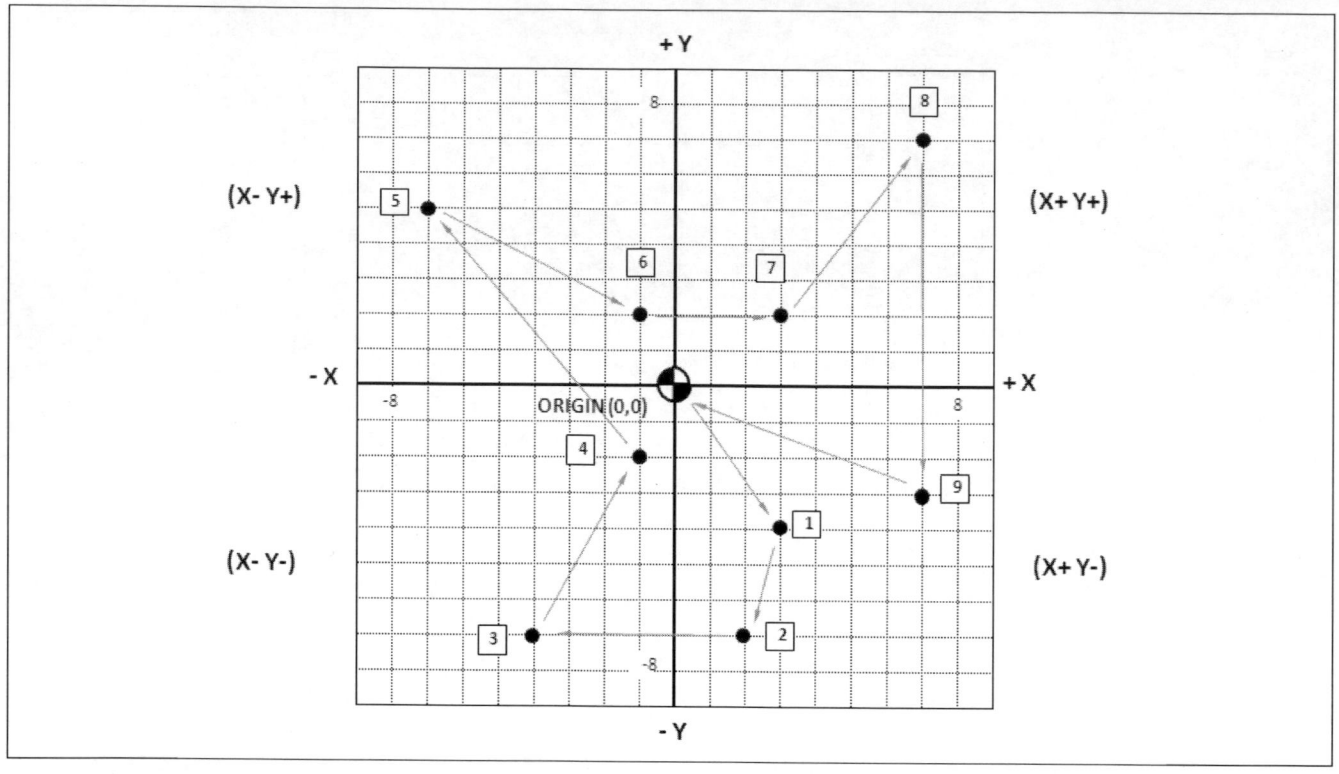

G90 ABSOLUTE PROGRAMMING

All axis motions are based on a fixed zero reference point, known as ABSOLUTE ZERO (part zero).
Each coordinate is in relation to this absolute zero using Cartesian Co-ordinates.

G91 INCREMENTAL PROGRAMMING

All axis motions are based on the distance to the next location.
Each coordinate is based on how far the cutter is to move from start to finish.

✎ ***STARTING AT THE POINT O (ORIGIN), DESCRIBE THE PATH FROM O THROUGH ALL 9 POINTS AND BACK TO THE POINT O USING G90 & G91***

G90	X	Y	G91	X	Y
O (Origin)			O → 1		
1			1 → 2		
2			2 → 3		
3			3 → 4		
4			4 → 5		
5			5 → 6		
6			6 → 7		
7			7 → 8		
8			8 → 9		
9			9 → O		

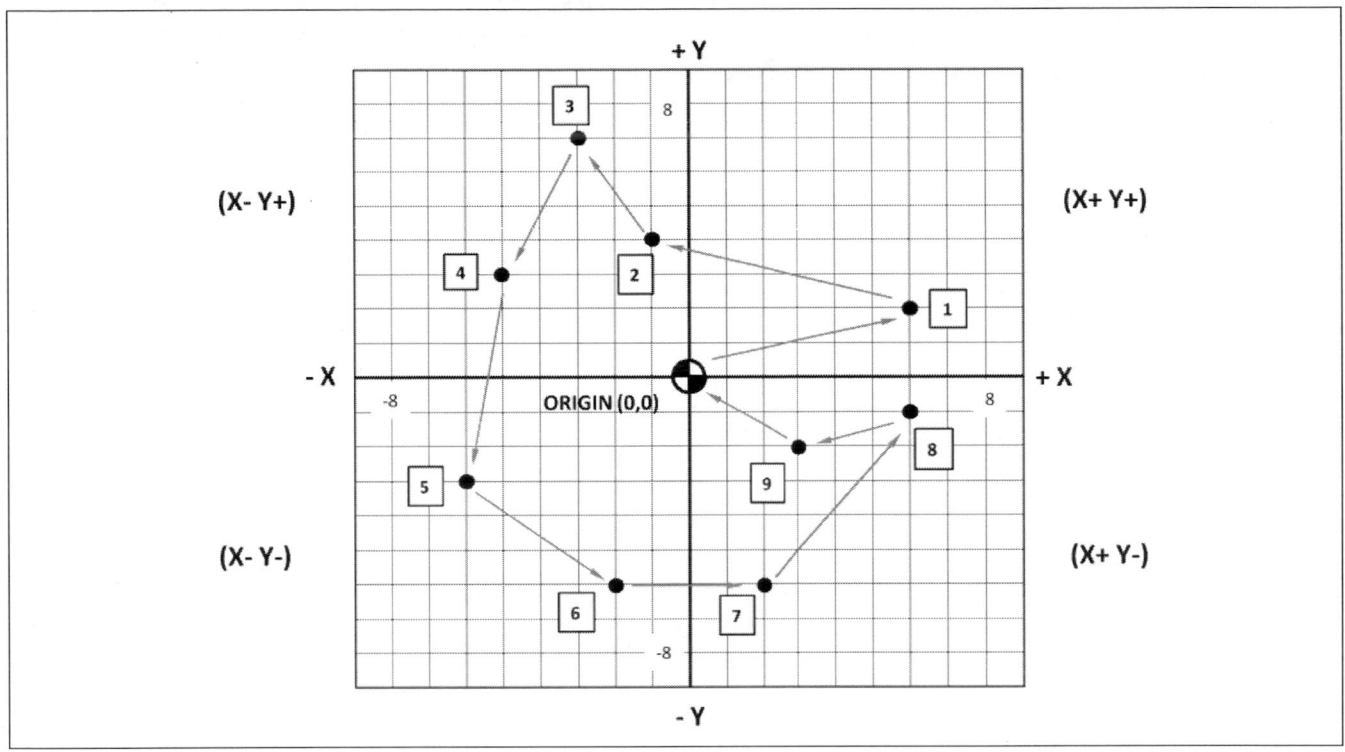

G90 ABSOLUTE PROGRAMMING

All axis motions are based on a fixed zero reference point, known as ABSOLUTE ZERO (part zero).
Each coordinate is in relation to this absolute zero using Cartesian Co-ordinates.

G91 INCREMENTAL PROGRAMMING

All axis motions are based on the distance to the next location.
Each coordinate is based on how far the cutter is to move from start to finish.

✏ ***STARTING AT THE POINT O (ORIGIN), DESCRIBE THE PATH FROM O THROUGH ALL 9 POINTS AND BACK TO THE POINT O USING G90 & G91***

G90	X	Y	G91	X	Y
O (Origin)			0 → 1		
1			1 → 2		
2			2 → 3		
3			3 → 4		
4			4 → 5		
5			5 → 6		
6			6 → 7		
7			7 → 8		
8			8 → 9		
9			9 → O		

Notes Page – please use this page to make notes:

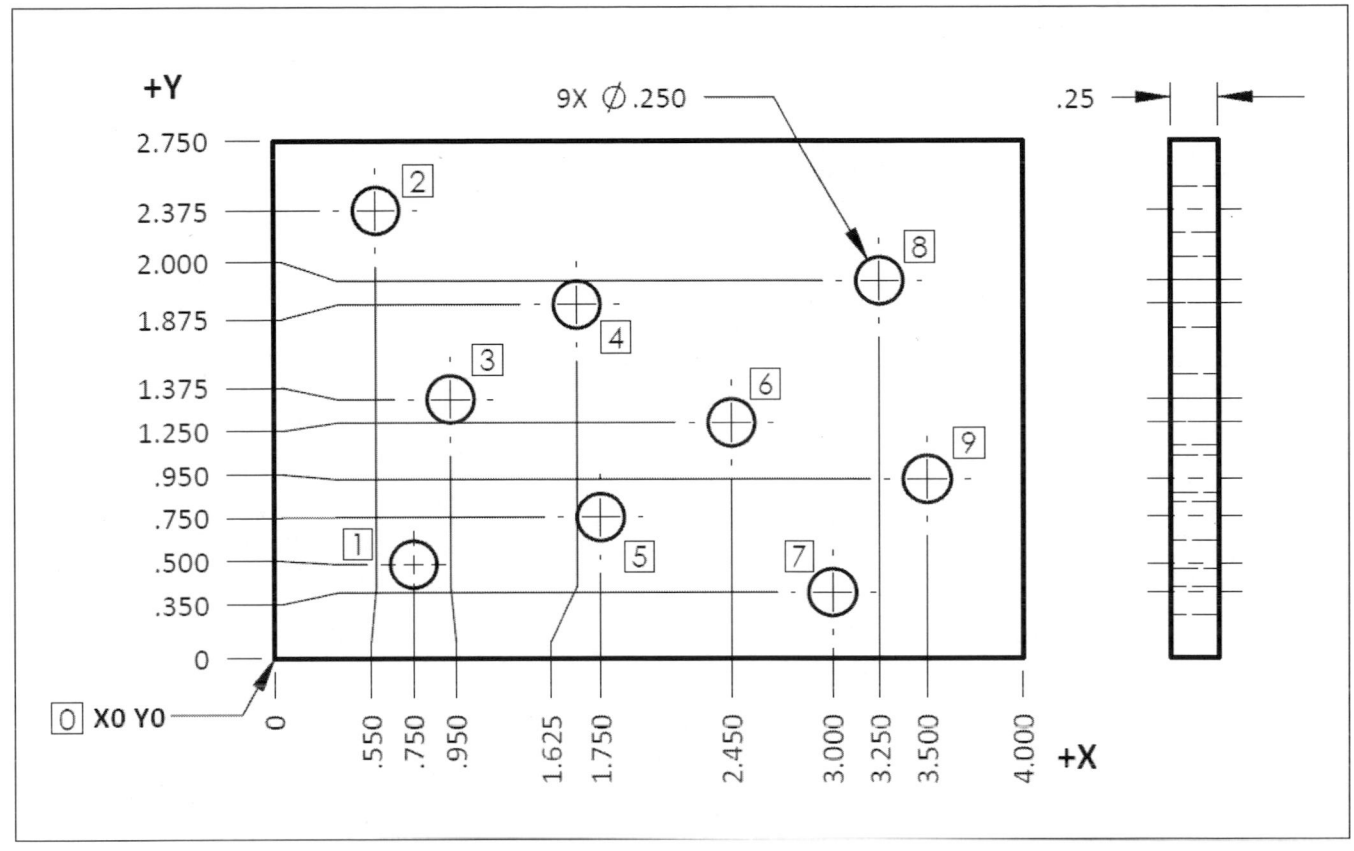

✏ **STARTING AT THE POINT O (ORIGIN), DESCRIBE THE PATH FROM O THROUGH ALL 9 POINTS AND BACK TO THE POINT O USING G90 & G91**

G90	X	Y	G91	X	Y
O (Origin)	0	0	O → 1	0.750	0.500
1	0.750	0.500	1 → 2	-0.200	1.875
2	0.550	2.375	2 → 3	0.400	-1.000
3	0.950	1.375	3 → 4		
4			4 → 5		
5			5 → 6		
6			6 → 7		
7			7 → 8		
8			8 → 9		
9			9 → O		

Notes Page – please use this page to make notes:

CNC PROGRAMMING WORKBOOK

CODE	FUNCTION
G00	Rapid traverse motion; This is used for non-cutting rapid moves of the machine axis, or rapid retract moves after cuts have been completed. Maximum rapid motion (I.P.M.) of a CNC Machine will vary dependent on machine model.
G01	Linear interpolation motion; Used for cutting in a straight line under a controlled feedrate. Maximum feed rate (I.P.M.) of a CNC Machine will vary depending on the model of the machine.
G02	Circular Interpolation, Clockwise
G03	Circular Interpolation, Counterclockwise
G04	Dwell
G17	Circular Motion XY Plane Selection
G20	Verify Inch Coordinate Positions
G21	Verify Metric Coordinate Positions
G28	Machine Home (Rapid traverse) G91 is required for rapid move to the G28 reference point.
G40	Cutter Compensation CANCEL

LESSON-2

INTRODUCTION TO CNC CODES

camInstructor

LESSON-2 - INTRODUCTION TO CNC CODES
AUTOMATIC TOOL CHANGER
STANDARD TOOL CAROUSEL

The CNC Machining Center used in this text is set-up with following tools. All program examples and exercises in this workbook are using the tools and tool numbers listed below.

Carousel #	Tool Description
1	0.125" Diameter Flat End Mill
2	0.250" Diameter Flat End Mill
3	0.375" Diameter Flat End Mill
4	0.500" Diameter Flat End Mill
5	0.750" Diameter Flat End Mill
6	0.375" Diameter Spot Drill
7	0.250" Diameter Drill
8	0.201" Diameter Drill – Number 7 drill
9	0.25"-20 UNC Tap
10	#4 Center Drill

CODE	FUNCTION
G00	Rapid traverse motion; This is used for non-cutting rapid moves of the machine axis, or rapid retract moves after cuts have been completed. Maximum rapid motion (I.P.M.) of a CNC Machine will vary dependent on machine model.
G01	Linear interpolation motion; Used for cutting in a straight line under a controlled feedrate. Maximum feed rate (I.P.M.) of a CNC Machine will vary depending on the model of the machine.
G02	Circular Interpolation, Clockwise
G03	Circular Interpolation, Counterclockwise
G04	Dwell
G17	Circular Motion XY Plane Selection
G20	Verify Inch Coordinate Positions
G21	Verify Metric Coordinate Positions
G28	Machine Home (Rapid traverse) G91 is required for rapid move to the G28 reference point.
G40	Cutter Compensation CANCEL
G41	Cutter Compensation LEFT of the programmed path
G42	Cutter Compensation RIGHT of the programmed path
G43	Tool Length Compensation
G49	Tool Length Compensation CANCEL
G53	Positions the machine axis relative to Machine Home. It is non modal.
G54	Work Coordinate #1 (Part zero offset location)
G80	Canned Cycle CANCEL
G81	Drill Canned Cycle
G82	Spot Drill Canned Cycle
G83	Peck Drill Canned Cycle
G84	Tapping Canned Cycle
G90	Absolute Programming Positioning
G91	Incremental Programming Positioning
G98	Canned Cycle Initial Point Return
G99	Canned Cycle Rapid (R) Plane Return

CODE	FUNCTION
M00	The M00 code is used for a Program Stop. The spindle stops and the coolant is turned off. Pressing CYCLE START again will continue the program.
M01	The M01 code is used for an Optional Program Stop command. Pressing the OPT STOP key on the control panel signals the machine to perform a stop command when the control reads an M01 command. It will then perform like an M00. Optional stops are useful when machining the first part to allow for inspection of the part as it is machined.
M03	Starts the spindle CLOCKWISE used for most machining. Must have a spindle speed defined. The M03 is used to turn the spindle on at the beginning of program or after a tool change.
M04	Starts the spindle COUNTERCLOCKWISE. Must have a spindle speed defined.
M05	STOPS the spindle. The M05 is used to turn the spindle off at the end of program or before a tool change. If the coolant is on, the M05 will turn it off.
M06	The tool change command along with a tool number will action a tool change. This command will automatically stop the spindle, Z-axis will move up to the machine zero position and the selected tool will be put in the spindle. The coolant pump will turn off right before executing the tool change.
M08	Coolant ON command.
M09	Coolant OFF command.
M30	Program End and Reset to the beginning of program.

Note: Only one "M" code can be used per line. And the M-codes will be the last command to be executed in a line, regardless of where it is located in that line.

%	Programs must begin and end with "%" depending on the type of control.
O00023	Letter "O" and up to a five digit program number. Blocks are always terminated by the ";" symbol: End of Block (EOB)
N10 G20	Nnn - Sequence Number G20 - Verify Inch
N20 G00 G17 G40 G49 G80 G90	G00 - Rapid Traverse G17 - X, Y Circular Plane Selection G40 - Cutter Compensation Cancel G49 - Tool Length Compensation Cancel G80 - Canned Cycle Cancel G90 - Absolute Programming	Startup Block (Machine Default Setting)
N30 T8 M06	T8 - Tool number #8 to be loaded into the spindle. M06 - Tool Change
N40 G00 G90 G54 X1.0 Y1.0 S4000 M03	G00 - Rapid Traverse G90 - Activates control to be in ABSOLUTE. G54 - Selects work coordinate offset system No. 1 X__ - Axis move to initial X position. Y__ - Axis move to initial Y position. S4000 - Spindle speed 4000 RPM for this tool. M03 - Turns the spindle on in a clockwise direction
N50 G43 H8 Z2. 0	G43 - Tool Length Compensation: Recognizes the tool length offset value stored in the Hnn code offset display register in the offset length display. H8 - Defines to the control the offset register the tool offset value is stored in. *** Tool Length offset # = Tool #*** Z2.0 - Informs the control to move from full spindle retract to this Z value and apply the tool length offset.

EXAMPLE OF PROGRAM **END BLOCKS**

N200 G00 Z2.0	G00 - Rapid Traverse Z2.0 – Retracts tool to 2.0 above part zero
N210 M05	M05 – Turn off spindle
N220 G28 G91 Z0 ** N220 G53 Z0*	G91 - Incremental Programming G28 - Machine Zero Return Z0 - Z axis in the up direction to machine zero	***Send to machine zero Z-axis first to avoid any crash.***
N230 G28 X0 Y0 ** N230 G53 X0 Y0*	G28 - Machine Zero Return X0 - X axis to machine zero Y0 - Y axis to machine zero	****G53 is another way to return to machine zero***
N240 M30	M30 – End of Program and Reset	

EXAMPLE OF PROGRAM **TOOL CHANGE LINES**

N100 G00 Z2.0	Rapid Traverse and Retracts tool to 2.0 above part zero
N110 M05	M05 – Turn off spindle
N120 G28 G91 Z0 ; / *N120 G53 Z0	Machine Zero Return - Z axis	***Send to machine zero Z-axis first to avoid any crash.***
N130 G28 X0 Y0 / *N130 G53 X0 Y0	Machine Zero Return - X, Y axis	
N140 M01	Optional Program Stop
N150 T9 M06	Tool Change - Tool # 9
N160 G00 G90 G54 X1.0 Y1.0 S4000 M03	Turn on the spindle and Rapid traverse to X1. Y1.
N170 G43 H9 Z2.0	Tool Length compensation for Tool #9 (H9)

*G53 - Positions the machine axis relative to Machine Home. It is non modal.

G00 RAPID TRAVERSE

This code is used for rapid motion of the cutter in air to traverse from one position to another as fast as possible. This code will work for all axis motion up to three axes at once.

This G00 code is modal and causes all the following blocks to be in rapid motion until another Group 01 code is specified. The actual rapid federate is dependent on the machine.

Generally, rapid motions "will not" be in a straight line. All the axes specified are moved at the maximum speed and will not necessarily complete each axis move at the same time. It activates each axis drive motor independently of each other and, as a result, the axis with the shortest move will reach its destination first. So ***you need to be careful of any obstructions to avoid with this type of rapid move.***

- G00 is used when you are positioning the cutter in 'fresh air'.

- Retracting from a hole you have drilled.

- Rapid traverse is not used when cutting the part.

- Used incorrectly, rapid traverse will break a cutter very easily.

G01 LINEAR INTERPOLATION

This G code provides for straight line (linear) motion with programmed feedrate for all axis motions from point to point. Motion can occur up to three axes at once.

All axes specified will start at the same time and proceed to their destination and arrive simultaneously at the specified feedrate.

To program a feedrate, the F command is used. The F command is modal and may be specified in a previous block.

G01 is used for
- Drilling a hole

- Machining a slot

- Machining a profile

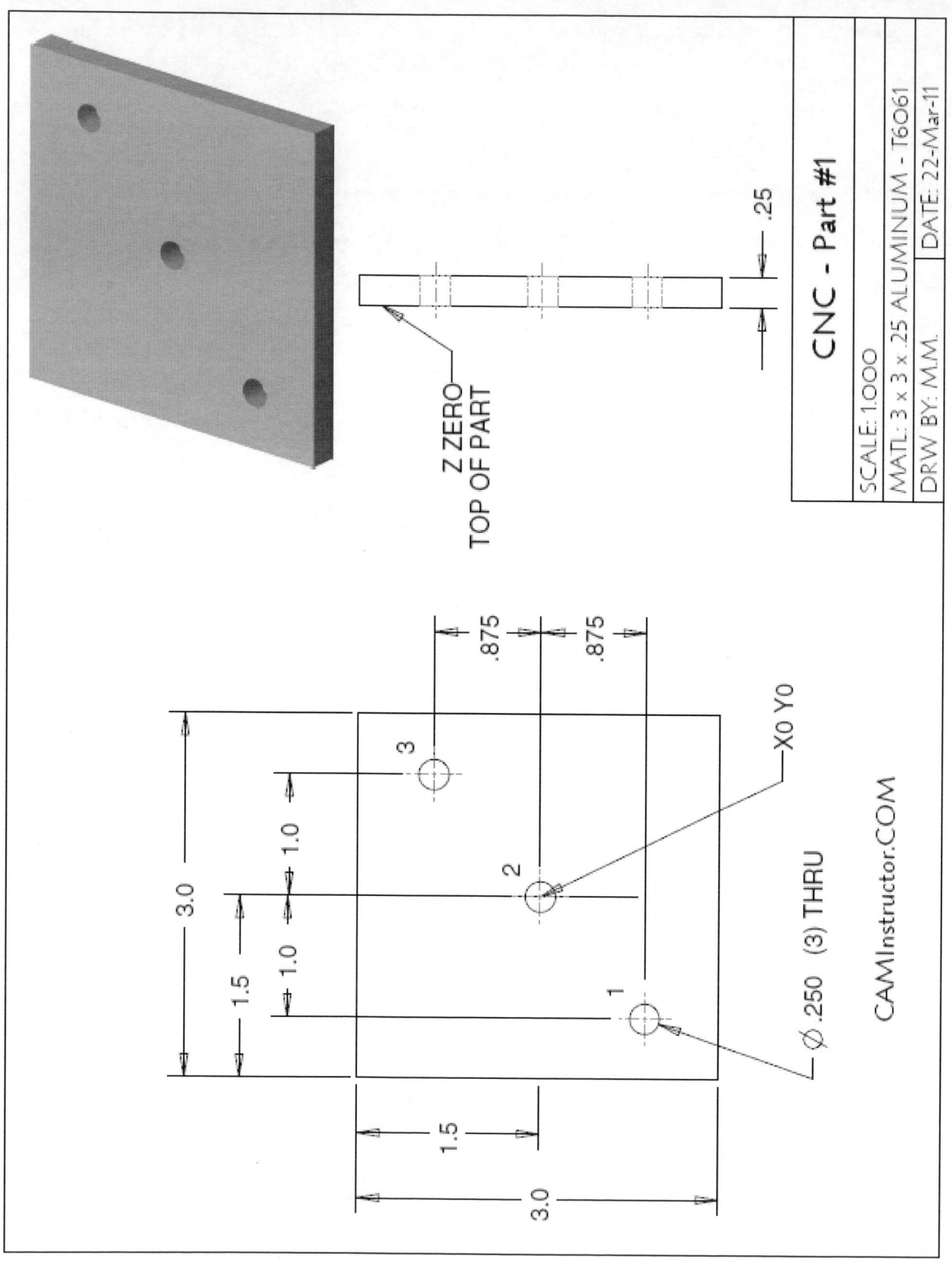

CNC - Part #1

SCALE: 1.000
MATL: 3 x 3 x .25 ALUMINUM - T6061
DRW BY: MM.   DATE: 22-Mar-11

Z ZERO
TOP OF PART

.25

.875
.875

3
2
1

X0 Y0

1.0
1.0
3.0
1.5

1.5
3.0

Ø .250 (3) THRU

CAMInstructor.COM

- **WORK OUT THE X AND Y COORDIANTES FOR HOLES 1,2 AND 3**
  - X0Y0 is at the centre of the part

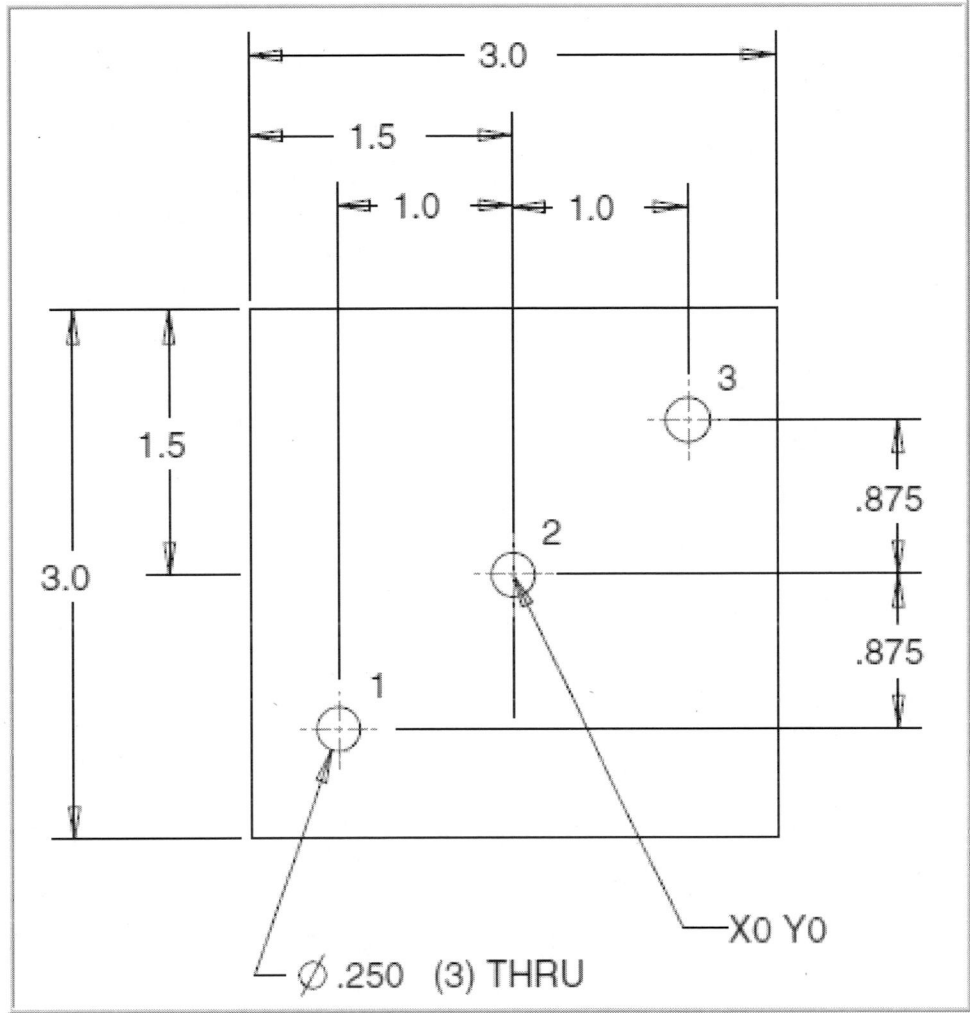

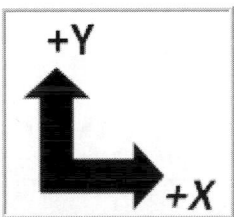

G90	X	Y
1		
2		
3		

- **PROGRAM TO _SPOT DRILL THE THREE HOLES ONLY_ USING A COMBINATION OF G00 AND G01 (CANNED CYCLE DRILL WILL BE USED LATER)**

  - Below is the program to spot drill the three holes with an explanation of each block
  - Use a 0.375" diameter Spot Drill Tool # 6
  - Spindle Speed = 2750 Feed rate = 11 IPM
  - Spot Drill Depth = Z-0.150"
  - X0Y0 is at the centre of the part
  - Z=0 is the top of the part.
  - Information inside the parenthesis ( ) is a comment.
  - The CNC control will ignore all text between the parenthesis

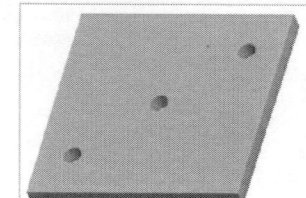

%		(Program must begin and end with a %)
O1		(Program #1 - CNC-PART-1-SPOT DRILLING ONLY)
N10	G20	(Inch programming)
N20	G00 G17 G40 G49 G80 G90 (MACHINE DEFAULT SETTING)	
N30	T06 M06	(T6-Select tool number 6 to be loaded M06-Activates the tool changer)
N40	G00 G90 G54 X-1.0 Y-0.875 S2750 M03 – (Rapid to the X and Y position and turn on the spindle at 2750 RPM)	
N50	G43 H06 Z0.1	(G43 - Activate the tool offset value stored in H06 and rapid to Z0.1)
N60	G01 Z-0.15 F11.0	(Hole #1 - Feed down to Z depth at 11 inches per minute)
N70	G00 Z0.1	(G00- Retract out of hole #1 at rapid to 0.1 above the top of the work piece)
N80	X0 Y0	(G00 is modal - Move at rapid in the X and Y axis to hole #2)
N90	G01 Z-0.15	(Hole #2 - Feed down to Z depth at 11 inches per minute, Feed rate is modal)
N100	G00 Z0.1	(G00- Retract out of hole #2 at rapid to 0.1 above the top of the work piece)
N110	X1.0 Y0.875	(G00 is modal - Move at rapid in the X and Y axis to hole #3)
N120	G01 Z-0.15	(Hole #3 - Feed down to Z depth at 11 inches per minute, Feed rate is modal)
N130	G53 G00 Z0 M05	(G53 – Machine Zero positioning, non modal. Rapid to machine zero in Z, switch spindle off)
N140	G53 X-15.0 Y0	(G53 – Rapid in relation to machine zero X-15.0 and Y0)
N150	M30	(Program end rewind program to the beginning)
%		(Program must begin and end with a %)

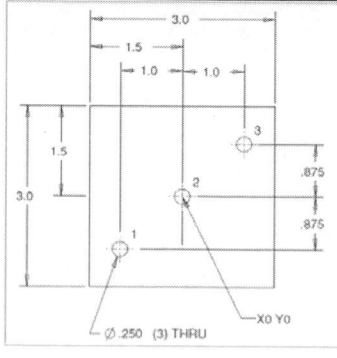

CNC Programming Workbook

Lesson-3

Creating CNC Programs - CNC Part #1

camInstructor

- ■ **PROGRAM TO <u>SPOT AND DRILL THE THREE HOLES</u> USING A COMBINATION OF G00 AND G01 (CANNED CYCLE WILL BE USED LATER)**
    - Below is the program to spot and drill the three holes with an explanation of each block
    - Use a 0.375" diameter Spot Drill Tool # 6
    - Spot Drill Spindle Speed = 2750 Feed rate = 11 IPM
    - Use a 0.250" diameter Drill Tool # 7
    - 0.250" diameter Drill Spindle Speed = 4500 Feed rate = 15 IPM
    - Spot Drill Depth = Z-0.150"
    - Drill Depth = Z-0.350"
    - X0Y0 is at the centre of the part
    - Z=0 is the top of the part.

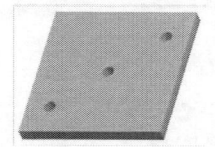

%	(Program must begin and end with a %)
O2	(Program #2 - CNC-PART-1-SPOT AND DRILLING)
N10 G20	(Inch programming)
N20 G00 G17 G40 G49 G80 G90	(MACHINE DEFAULT SETTING)
(SPOT DRILL 0.25" HOLES)	
N30 T06 M06	(T6-Select tool number 6 to be loaded M06-Activates the tool changer)
N40 G00 G90 G54 X-1.0 Y-0.875 S2750 M03	(Rapid to the X and Y position of Hole #1 and turn on the spindle at 2750 RPM)
N50 G43 H06 Z0.1	(G43 - Activate the tool offset value stored in H06 and rapid to Z0.1)
N60 G01 Z-0.15 F11.0	(Hole #1 - Feed down to Z depth at 11 inches per minute)
N70 G00 Z0.1	(G00- Retract out of hole #1 at rapid to 0.1 above the top of the work piece)
N80 X0 Y0	(G00 is modal - Move at rapid in the X and Y axis to Hole #2)
N90 G01 Z-0.15	(Hole #2 - Feed down to Z depth at 11 inches per minute, Feed rate is modal)
N100 G00 Z0.1	(G00- Retract out of hole #2 at rapid to 0.1 above the top of the work piece)
N110 X1.0 Y0.875	(G00 is modal - Move at rapid in the X and Y axis to hole #3)
N120 G01 Z-0.15	(Hole #3 - Feed down to Z depth at 11 inches per minute, Feed rate is modal)
N130 G53 G00 Z0 M05	(G53 – Machine Zero positioning, non modal. Rapid to machine zero in Z, switch spindle off)
N140 G53 X-15.0 Y0	(G53 – Rapid in relation to machine zero X-15.0 and Y0)
(DRILL 0.25" HOLES)	
N160 T07 M06	(T7-Select tool number 7 to be loaded M06-Activates the tool changer)
N170 G00 G90 G54 X-1.0 Y-0.875 S4500 M03	(Rapid to the X and Y position of Hole #1 and turn on the spindle at 4500 RPM)
N180 G43 H07 Z0.1	(G43 - Activate the tool offset value stored in H07 and rapid to Z0.1)
N190 G01 Z-0.35 F15.0	(Hole #1 - Feed down to Z depth at 15 inches per minute through part)
N200 G00 Z0.1	(G00- Retract out of hole #1 at rapid to 0.1 above the top of the work piece)

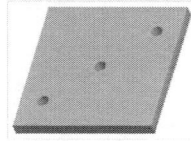

N210 X0 Y0	(G00 is modal - Move at rapid in the X and Y axis to hole #2)
N220 G01 Z-0.35	(Hole #2 - Feed down to Z depth, at 15 inches per minute, Feed rate is modal)
N230 G00 Z0.1	(G00- Retract out of hole #2 at rapid to 0.1 above the top of the work piece)
N240 X1.0 Y0.875	(G00 is modal - Move at rapid in the X and Y axis to hole #3)
N250 G01 Z-0.35	(Hole #3 - Feed down to Z depth at 15 inches per minute, Feed rate is modal)
N260 G53 G00 Z0 M05	(G53 – Machine Zero positioning, non modal. Rapid to machine zero in Z, switch spindle off)
N270 G53 X-15.0 Y0	(G53 – Rapid in relation to machine zero X-15.0 and Y0)
N270 M30	(Program end rewind program to the beginning)
%	(Program must begin and end with a %)

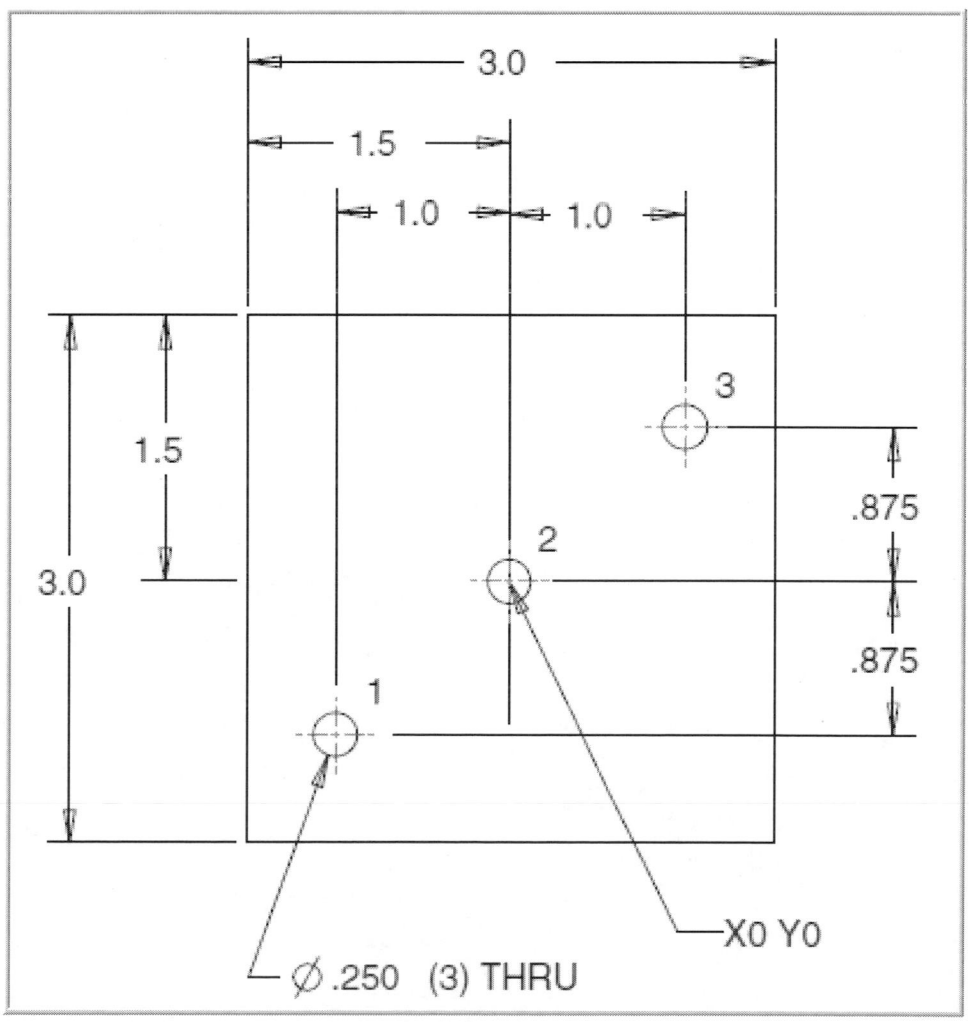

CNC Programming
Workbook

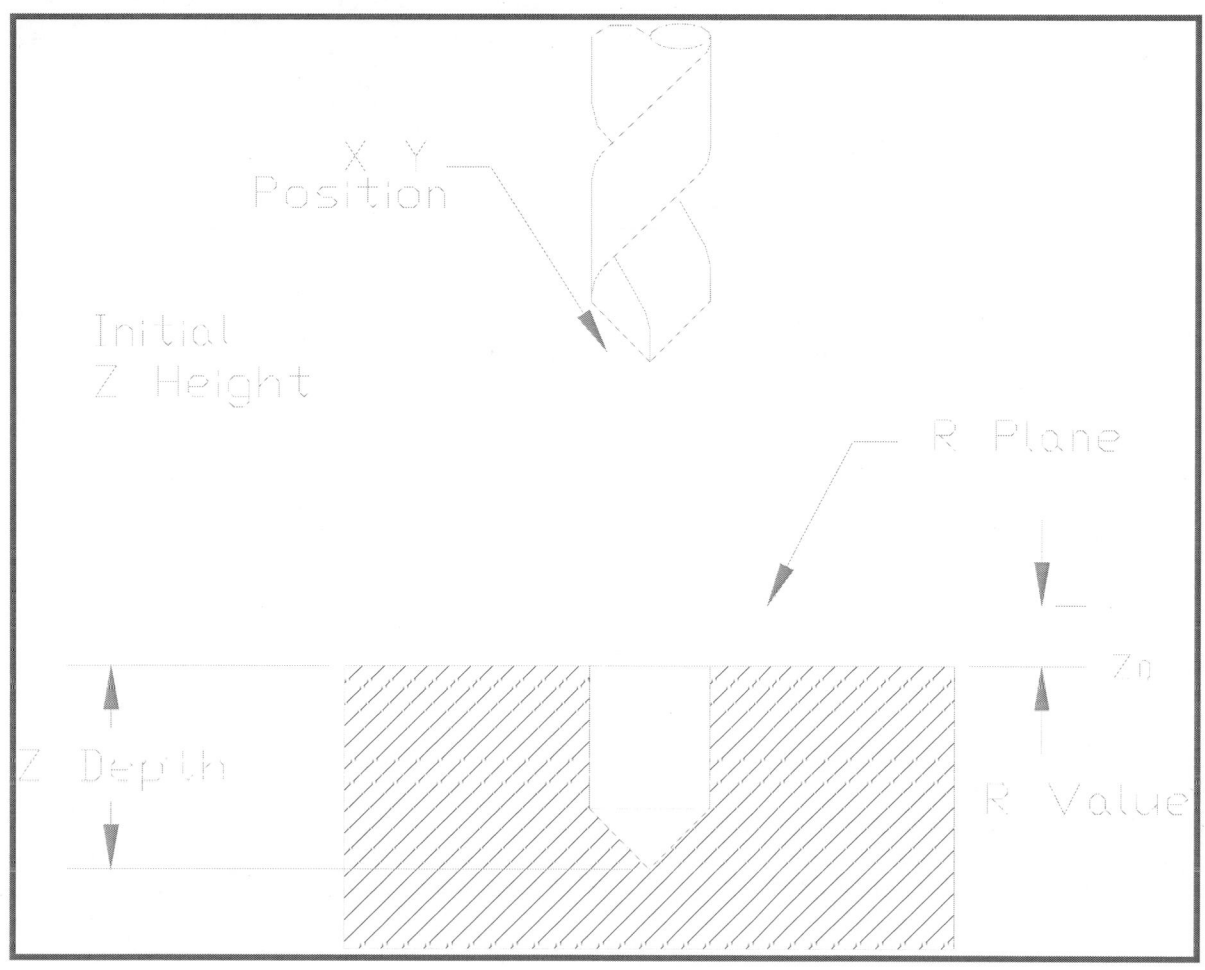

Lesson-4

Drilling Using Canned Cycles

camInstructor

G80 CANCEL CANNED CYCLE

A canned cycle permits multiple function programming on one block.

A canned cycle is canceled with G80.

G81 CANNED CYCLE DRILL

Format: G99 G81 Z-0.625 R0.1 F10.

X   Rapid X location (Optional)
Y   Rapid Y location (Optional)
Z   Z-depth (Feed to Z-depth starting from R Plane)
R   R-Plane (Rapid point to start feeding)
F   Feed rate in inches/min

This G code permits the inclusion of multiple axis motions on one block of program. It is used to reduce the length of program. The figure below shows the axis motions that are included with a Canned Cycle Drill.

All Z axis motions are in ABSOLUTE with any other axis motions unaffected.

In a canned cycle drill, the cutter moves at rapid to the X and Y, then to a height above the part at rapid rate to the R Plane, which is a point above the work surface. From the R Plane the cutter feeds to the Z-depth at the specified feedrate. When the cutter reaches the Z depth, it retracts at rapid rate to the R Plane. **G99** *returns the tool to the R Plane after each hole,* **G98** *returns the tool to the initial starting plane.*

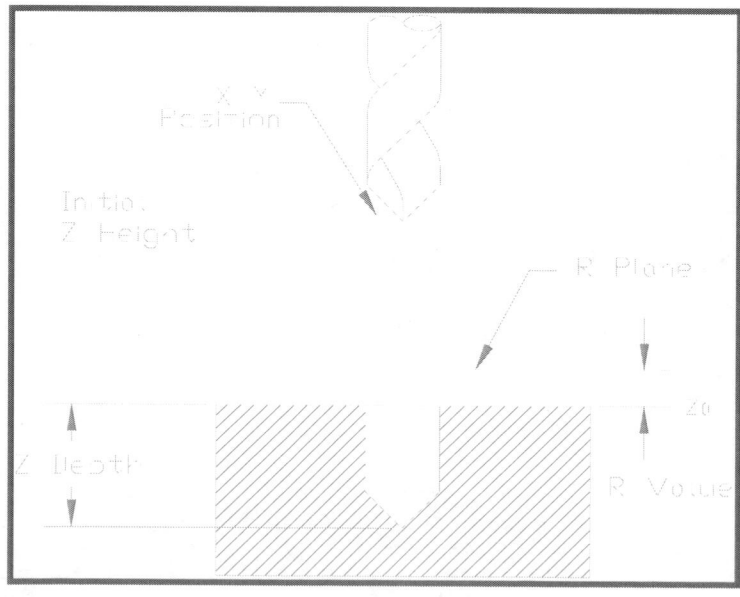

G83 DEEP HOLE PECK DRILL CANNED CYCLE

Format :   **G99 G83 Z-2.5 Q0.5 R0.1 F10.**   /   **G99 G83 Z-2.18 I0.5 J0.1 K0.2 R0.1 F9.**

- **X***   Rapid X-axis location
- **Y***   Rapid Y-axis location
- **Z**   Z-depth (feed to Z-depth starting from R plane)
- **Q***   Pecking equal incremental depth amount (if I, J and K are not used)
- **I***   Size of first peck depth (if Q is not used)
- **J***   Amount reducing each peck after first peck depth (if Q is not used)
- **K***   Minimum peck depth (if Q is not used)
- **P**   Dwell time at Z-depth
- **R**   R-plane (rapid point to start feeding)
- **F**   Feed rate in inches (mm) per minute
  - * Indicates optional

This G code is similar to G81 but is used for drilling when the tool must be withdrawn periodically to allow chips to be removed from the hole.

This cycle allows the tool to rapid to the R Plane, feeds towards the Z depth in increments (traversing to the R Plane and back to the point where drilling was interrupted after each increment) until the tool reaches the final Z depth.

- **CREATE THE PROGRAM TO _SPOT AND DRILL THE THREE HOLES_ USING CANNED CYCLE G81**
  - Use a 0.375" diameter Spot Drill Tool # 6
  - Spot Drill Spindle Speed = 2750 Feed rate = 11 IPM
  - Use a 0.250" diameter Drill Tool # 7
  - 0.250" diameter Drill Spindle Speed = 4500 Feed rate = 15 IPM
  - Spot Drill Depth = Z-0.150"
  - Drill Depth = Z-0.350"
  - X0Y0 is at the centre of the part
  - Z=0 is the top of the part.

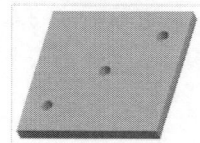

%	(Program must begin and end with a %)
O3	(Program #3 - CNC-PART-1-SPOT AND DRILLING USING CANNED CYCLE DRILL G81)
N10 G20	(Inch programming)
N20 G00 G17 G40 G49 G80 G90 (MACHINE DEFAULT SETTING)	
N30 T06 M06	(T6-Select tool number 6 to be loaded M06-Activates the tool changer)
N40 G00 G90 G54 X-1.0 Y-0.875 S2750 M03	(Rapid to the X and Y position of Hole #1 and turn on the spindle at 2750 RPM)
N50 G43 H06 Z0.1	(G43 - Activate the tool offset value stored in H06 and rapid to Z0.1)
N60 G99 G81 Z-0.15 R0.1 F11.0	(Hole #1 – G81 - Feed down to Z depth at 11 inches per minute, and then retract at rapid to Z0.1, this is the R0.1 value. G99 returns the drill tip to the R value after drilling each hole)
N70 X0. Y0.	(Hole #2 - Move at rapid in the X and Y axis to Hole #2. Feed down to Z depth at 11 inches per minute and then retract at rapid to Z0.1)
N80 X1.0 Y.875	(Hole #3 - Move at rapid in the X and Y axis to Hole #3. Feed down to Z depth at 11 inches per minute and then retract at rapid to Z0.1)
N90 G80	(Cancel Canned Cycle Drill)
N100 G53 G00 Z0 M05	(G53 – Rapid to machine zero in Z, switch spindle off)
N110 G53 X-15.0 Y0	(G53 – Rapid in relation to machine zero X-15.0 and Y0)
(DRILL 0.25" HOLES)	
N120 T07 M06	(T7-Select tool number 7 to be loaded M06-Activates the tool changer)
N130 G00 G90 G54 X-1.0 Y-0.875 S4500 M03	(Rapid to the X and Y position of Hole #1 and turn on the spindle at 4500 RPM)
N140 G43 H07 Z0.1	(G43 - Activate the tool offset value stored in H07 and rapid to Z0.1)

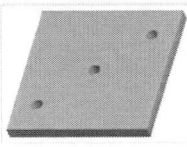

N150 G99 G81 Z-0.35 R0.1 F15.0	(Hole #1 – G81 - Feed down to Z depth at 15 inches per minute, and then retract at rapid to Z0.1, this is the R0.1 value. G99 returns the drill tip to the R value after drilling each hole)
N160 X0. Y0.	(Hole #2 - Move at rapid in the X and Y axis to Hole #2. Feed down to Z depth at 15 inches per minute and then retract at rapid to Z0.1)
N170 X1.0 Y.875	(Hole #3 - Move at rapid in the X and Y axis to Hole #3. Feed down to Z depth at 15 inches per minute and then retract at rapid to Z0.1)
N180 G80	(Cancel Canned Cycle Drill)
N190 G53 G00 Z0 M05	(G53 – Rapid to machine zero in Z, switch spindle off)
N200 G53 X-15.0 Y0	(G53 – Rapid in relation to machine zero X-15.0 and Y0)
N210 M30	(Program end rewind program to the beginning)
%	(Program must begin and end with a %)

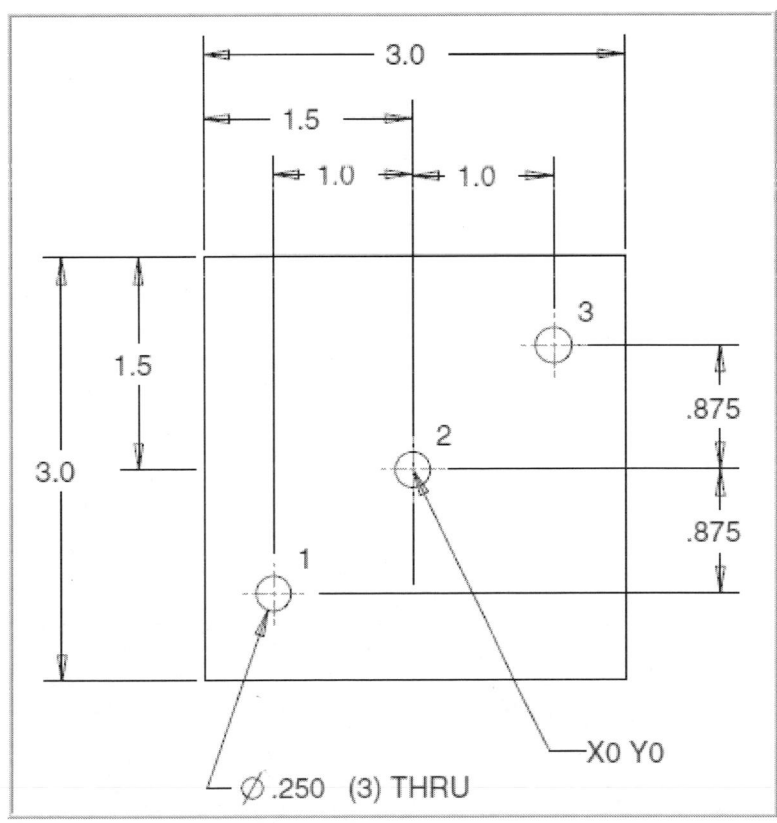

- ***IDENTIFY SOME OF THE COMMON PROBLEMS THAT COULD RESULT IN A SCRAPPED PART***

- Do you have X0 Y0 Z0 in the correct position?
- Is the spindle switched on and off at the appropriate time
- Did you use the correct X and Y coordinates for the holes?
- Did you use the correct tool numbers?
- Did you use the correct tool length offset number (H??) for the tool?
- Did you cancel any canned cycles with G80?
- Are the feed-rates correct?
- Is the Z depth in the canned cycle block set to a negative value?
- Is the R value in the canned cycle block set to a positive value?
- What is the difference between Z2 and Z2.0? No decimal point???
- What is the difference between F10 and F10.0? No decimal point???
- What else?

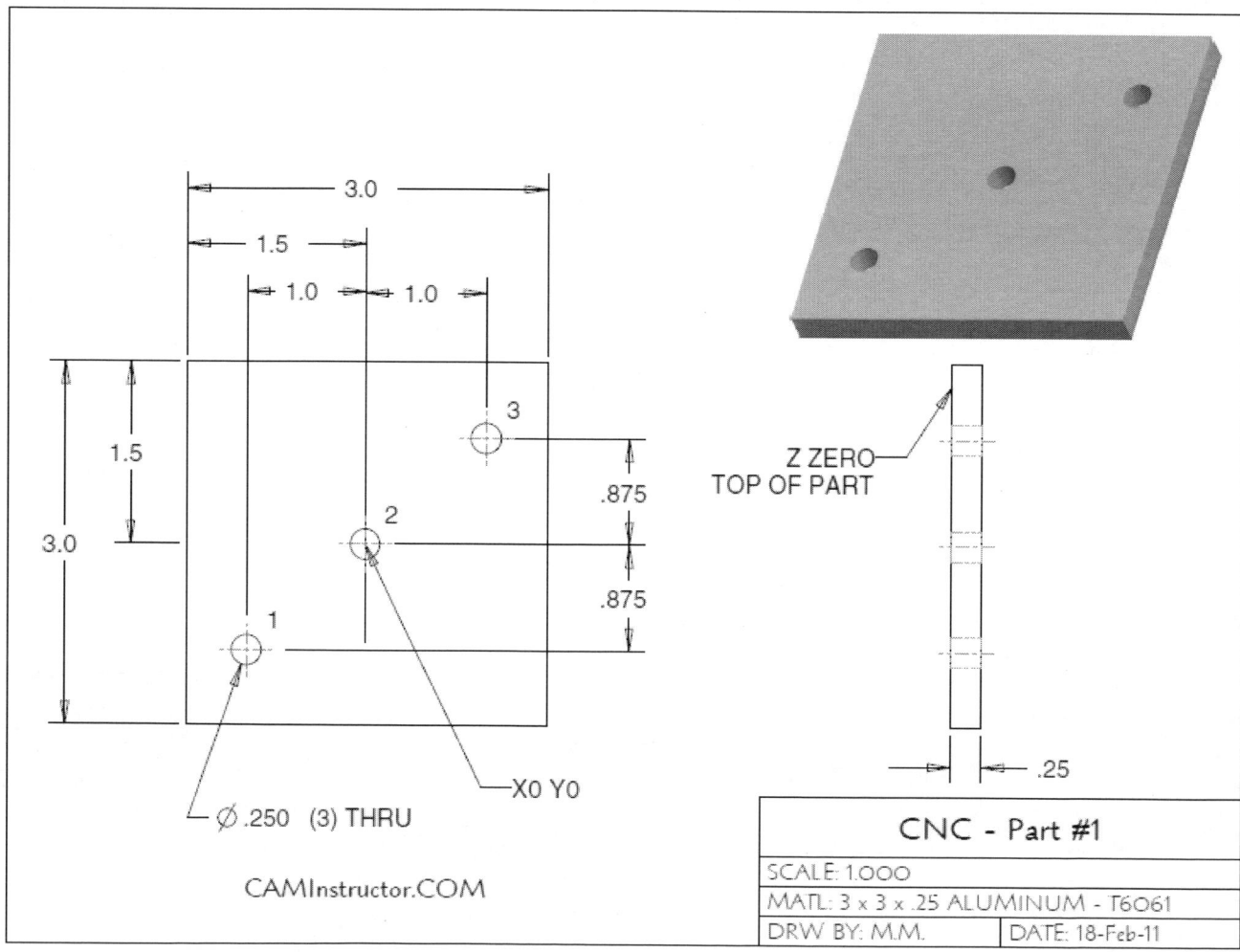

CNC PROGRAMMING
WORKBOOK

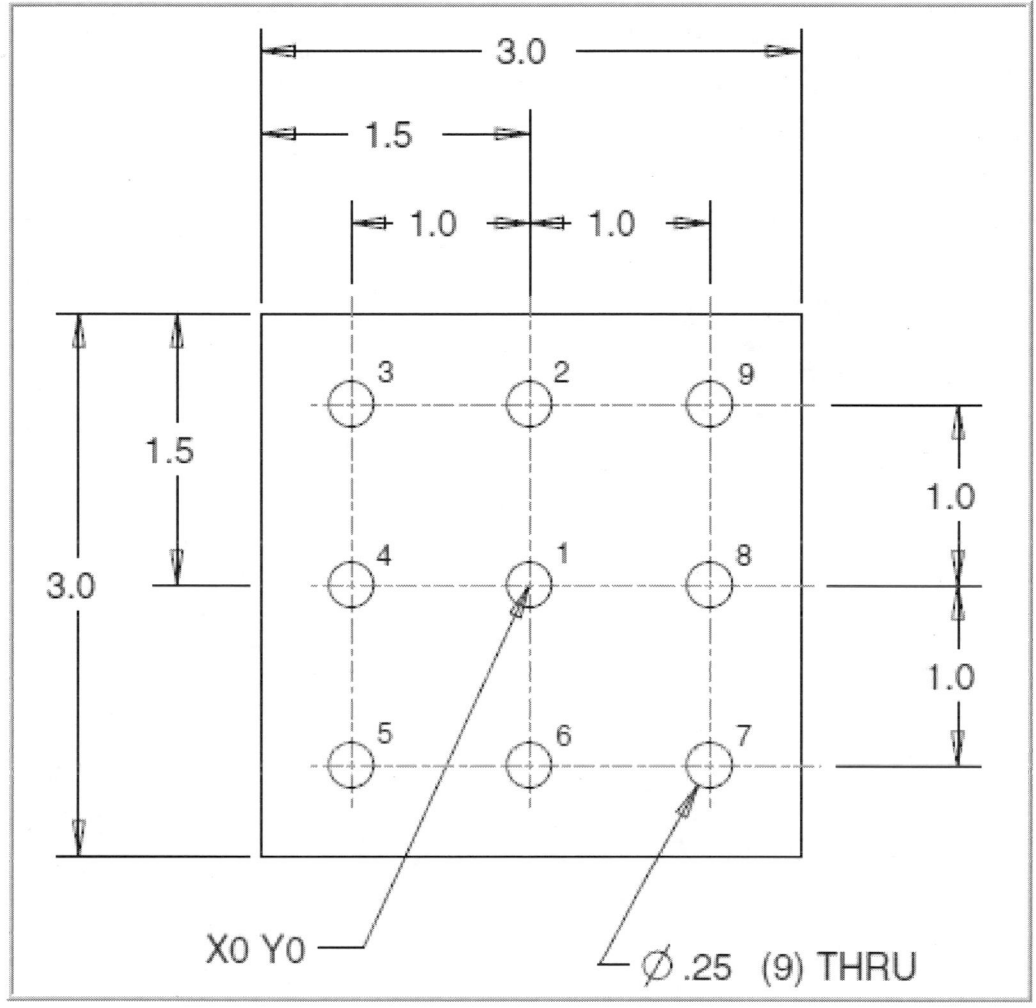

MILL-LESSON-5
DRILLING USING CANNED CYCLES - CONTINUED

camInstructor

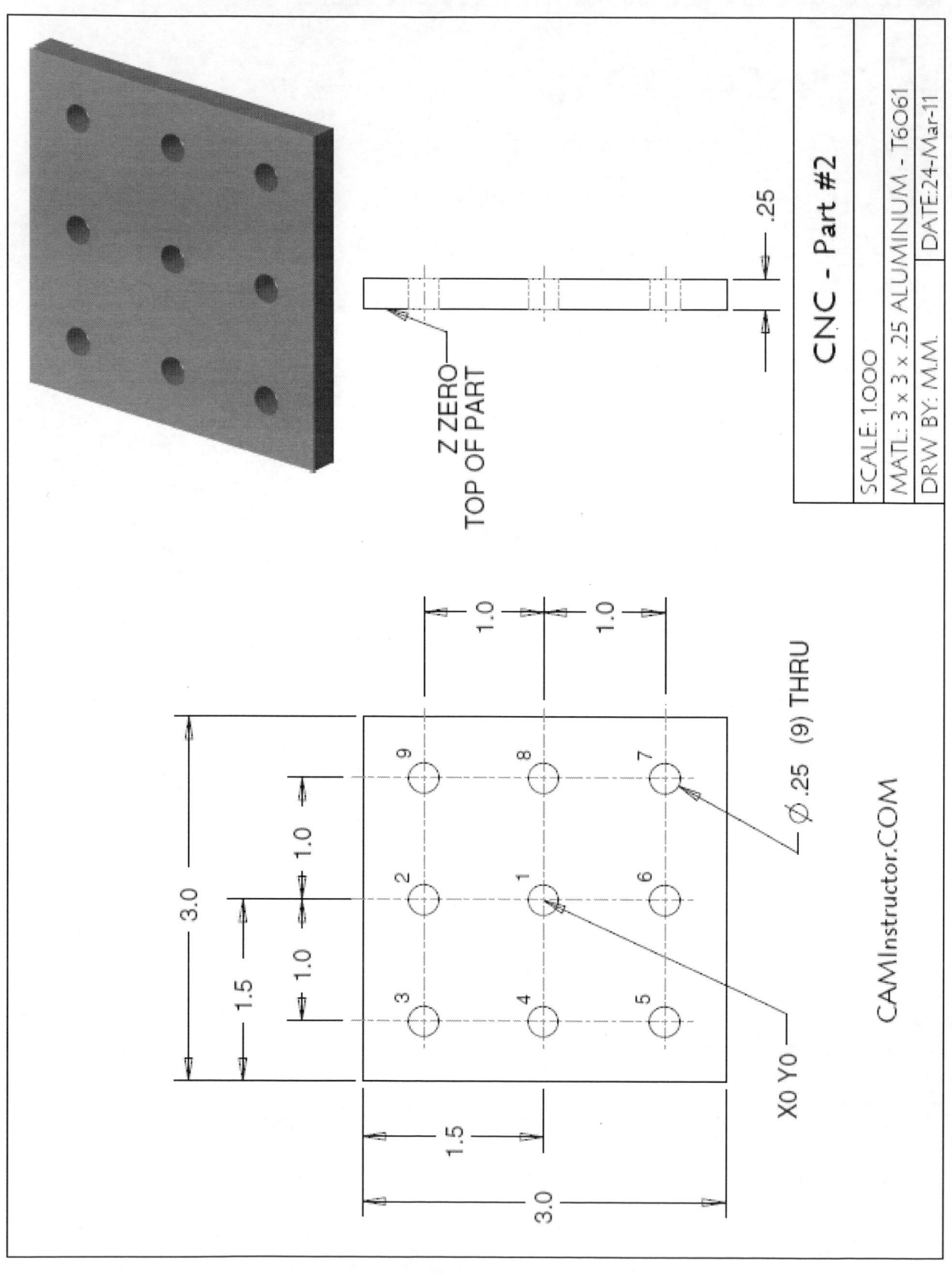

CNC - Part #2

SCALE: 1.000
MATL: 3 x 3 x .25 ALUMINUM - T6061
DRW BY: MM.   DATE:24-Mar-11

Z ZERO
TOP OF PART

.25

Ø.25 (9) THRU

CAMInstructor.COM

X0 Y0

1.0
1.0

3.0
1.5
1.0
1.0

1.5
3.0

- ### *WORK OUT THE ABSOLUTE COORDINATES FOR THE NINE HOLES*
  - X0Y0 is at the centre of the part

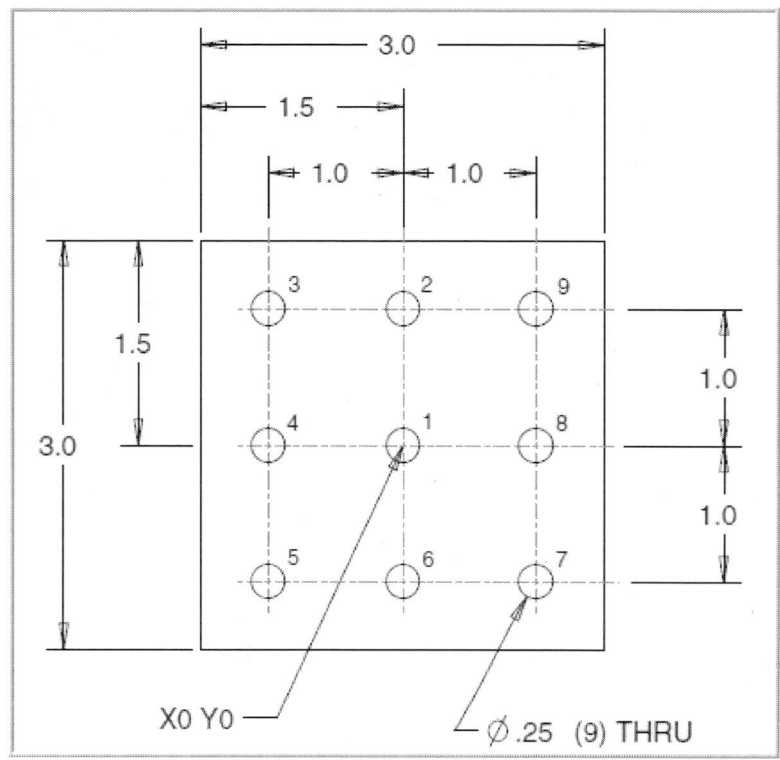

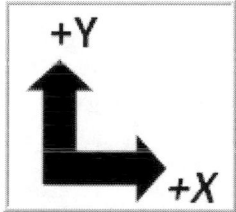

G90	X	Y
1		
2		
3		
4		
5		
6		
7		
8		
9		

- **_CREATE THE PROGRAM TO <u>SPOT AND DRILL THE NINE HOLES</u> USING CANNED CYCLE G81_**
  - Use a 0.375" diameter Spot Drill Tool # 6
  - Spot Drill Spindle Speed = 2750 Feed rate = 11 IPM
  - Use a 0.250" diameter Drill Tool # 7
  - 0.250" diameter Drill Spindle Speed = 4500 Feed rate = 15 IPM
  - Spot Drill Depth = Z-0.150"
  - Drill Depth = Z-0.350"
  - X0Y0 is at the centre of the part
  - Z=0 is the top of the part.
  - Type up your program and check it for correctness using the Backplot software.

%	
O4	(Program #4 - CNC-PART-2-SPOT AND DRILLING USING CANNED CYCLE DRILL G81)
N10	G20
N20	G00 G17 G40 G49 G80 G90 (MACHINE DEFAULT SETTING)
N30	

- ***Use Windows Notepad to type up your CNC program***
  1. Launch Windows Notepad **Start>All Programs>Accessories>Notepad**.

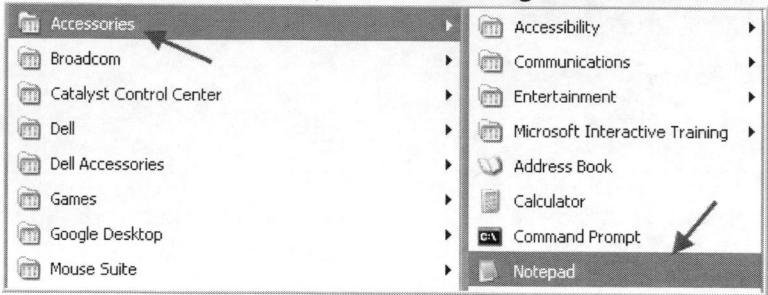

  2. Select **File Save As...**

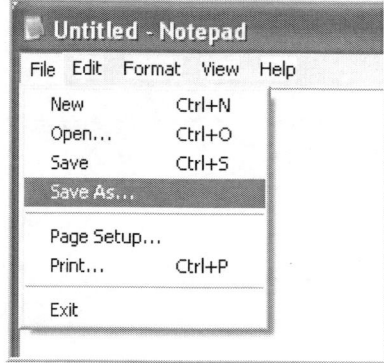

  3. **Browse** to where you would like to save this file.
  4. Open up the **Save as type** drop down and change to **All files**.
  5. **Encoding** should be set to **ANSI**.
  6. In the **File name** section enter **CNC-PART-2.NC** This will give this file an extension of **.NC**
  7. Click on the Save button

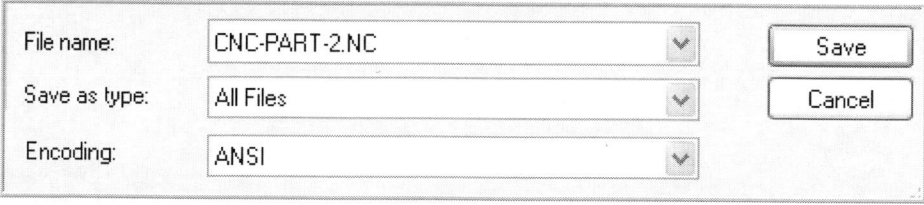

  8. Start typing your program, **ALL CAPITALS** for the CNC program codes. Please note on the second line of this program **O4** this is a **letter O**.

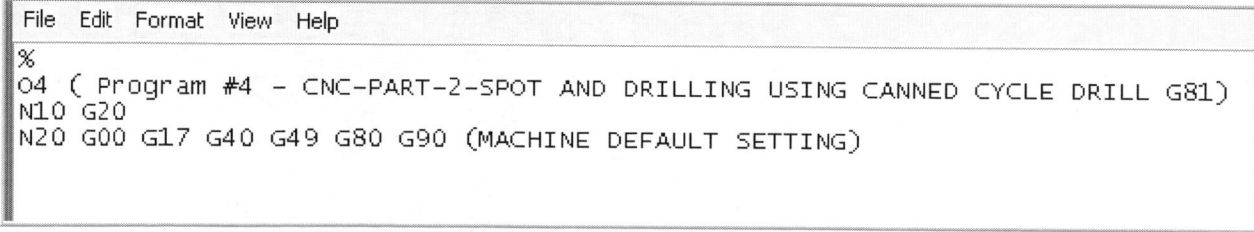

```
File  Edit  Format  View  Help
%
O4 ( Program #4 - CNC-PART-2-SPOT AND DRILLING USING CANNED CYCLE DRILL G81)
N10 G20
N20 G00 G17 G40 G49 G80 G90 (MACHINE DEFAULT SETTING)
```

9. When you have completed typing your program Save your file, File>**Save** or the shortcut **Ctrl+S**.

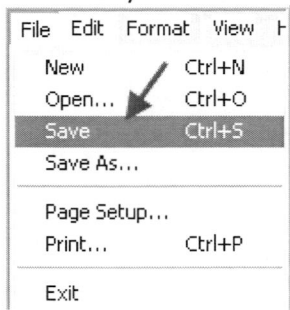

- **Now you can check for any Letter O's in your CNC program. Please Note there should not be any letter O's in your CNC program, G00 is "G Zero Zero" not G Letter O!**

10. Select **Edit>Find**.

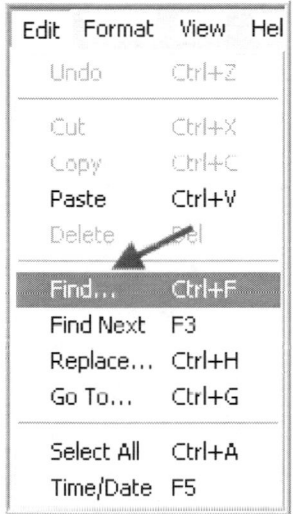

11. Type in the **Letter O** in the **Find what:** space. Now hit the Find Next button. There will be some letter O's in your program, for example the Letter O in the program number at the start of the program and any notes you have in your program enclosed by parenthesis ( ). But for the coding no letter O's.

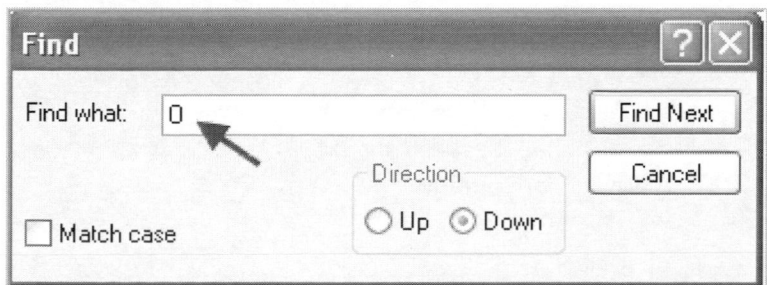

12. I f you do find any letter O's change them to a Zero.

13. When you have checked your program select **File>Save** your file or the shortcut **Ctrl+S**.

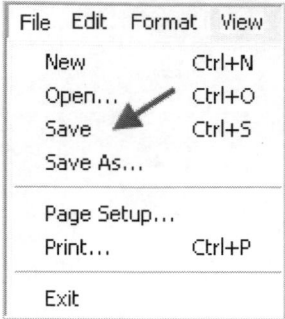

14. You may require a print of your CNC program to do this select **File>Print** or the shortcut **Ctrl+P**.
15. Select which printer you wish to send the file to and then hit the **Print** button

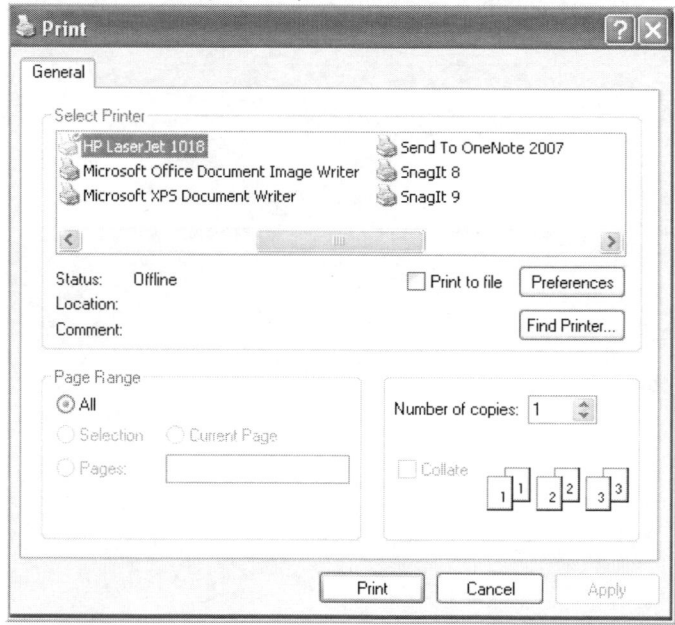

16. To open your CNC program at a later date launch Windows Notepad.
    Start>All Programs>Accessories>Notepad.
17. Select **File>Open**.

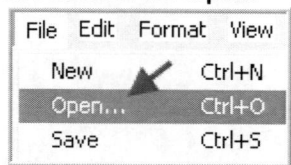

18. Change the **Files of type**: to **All Files** and browse for your CNC program.

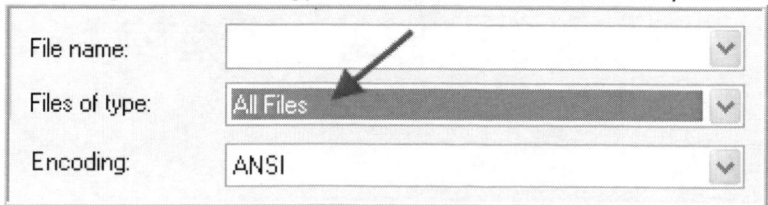

- ***Use Discriminator Backplot software to check for correctness***

Note: If you do not have Discriminator installed on your computer please go to the last page of the appendix for installation instructions.

1. After typing up your program in Notepad launch the Discriminator application by clicking on the icon on your desktop or **Start>All Programs>Discriminator> Discriminator**

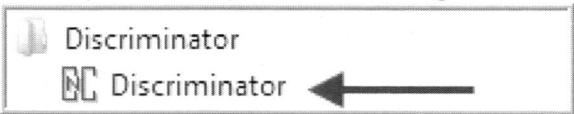

2. Click **OK** to any warnings you receive.
3. Click on **File>Open** and browse to your file location and select the CNC file to plot.

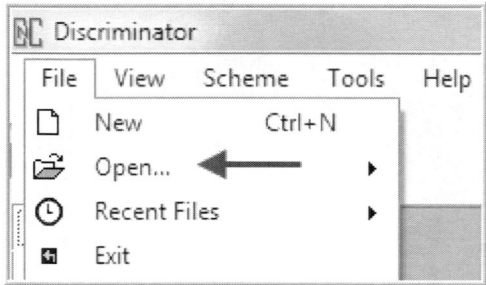

4. After selecting the CNC file it opens up in a separate window.

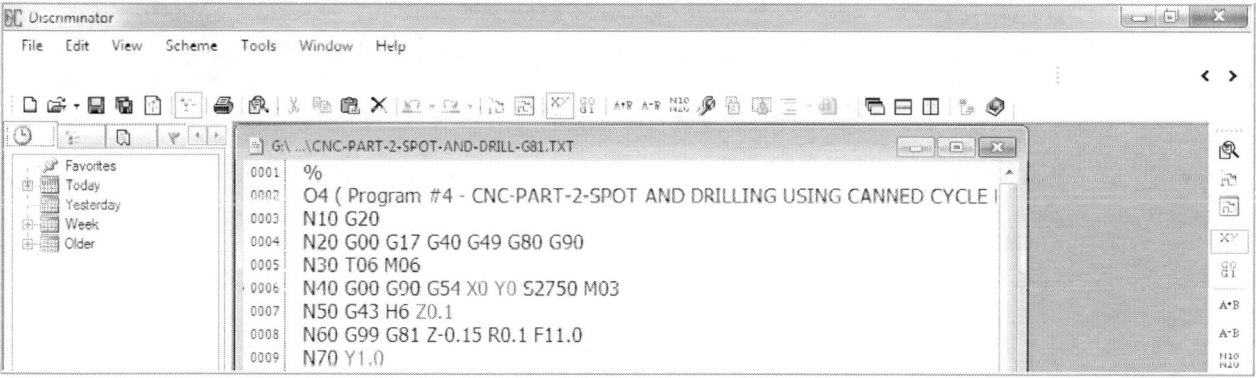

5. Now click on the show graphics icon 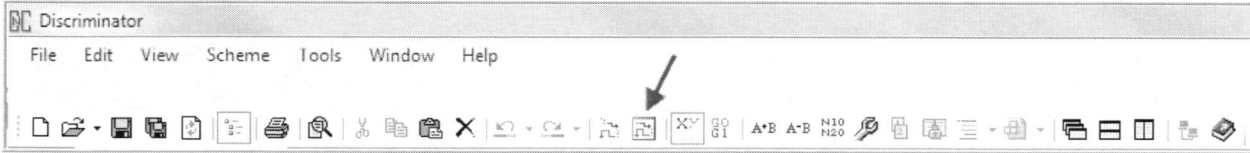 at the toolbar at the top of the screen to launch a plot of your CNC file.

6. When the plot screen opens up hit the **Maximize** button.

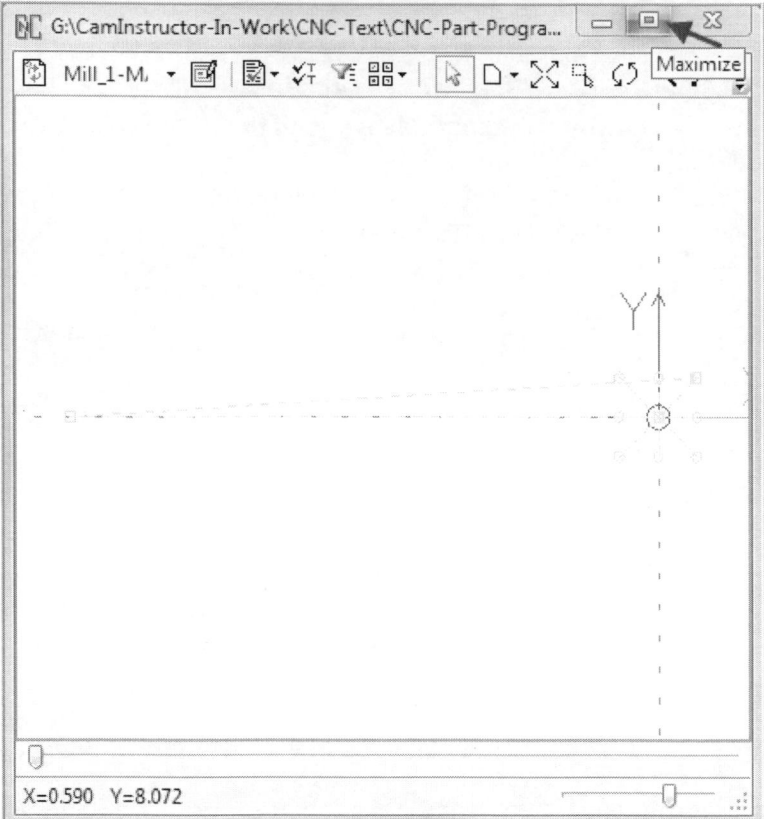

7. On the top toolbar select the icon to **View Fit**.

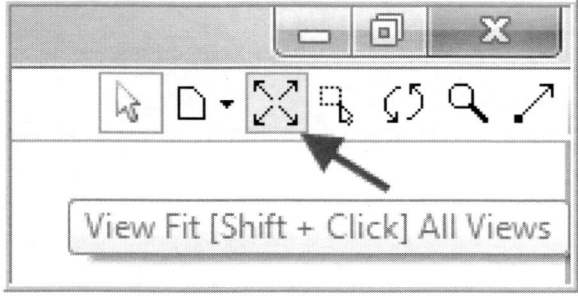

8. You plot should appear as below. The point on the left of the screen shot below is the G53 X-15.0 Y0 movement in the program.

9. Click the right mouse button on the main graphics plot screen and select **Views>Front**.

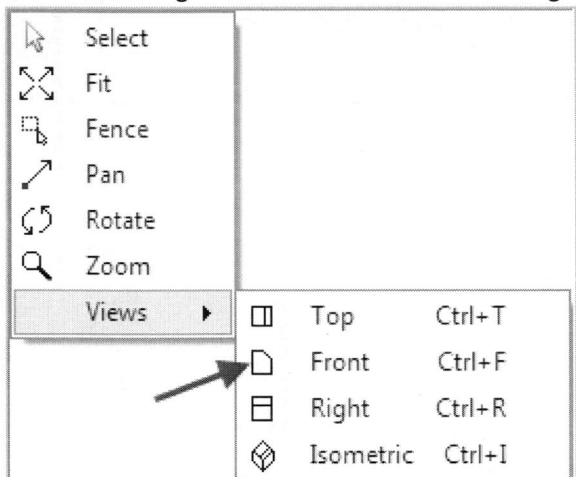

10. Return to a Top view by clicking the right mouse button on the main graphics plot screen and select **Views>Top**.

11. Experiment with the various display functions at the top right of the screen.

12. Review and experiment with the various toolbar options.

13. You can use **Discriminator** instead of Windows Notepad to type up your CNC program. Select the **New document** icon to create a new file and type up your program in the new document window.

- *PART #3 IS SIMILAR TO PART #2 BUT HAS DIFFERENT DIMENSIONS FOR THE HOLE CENTRES*

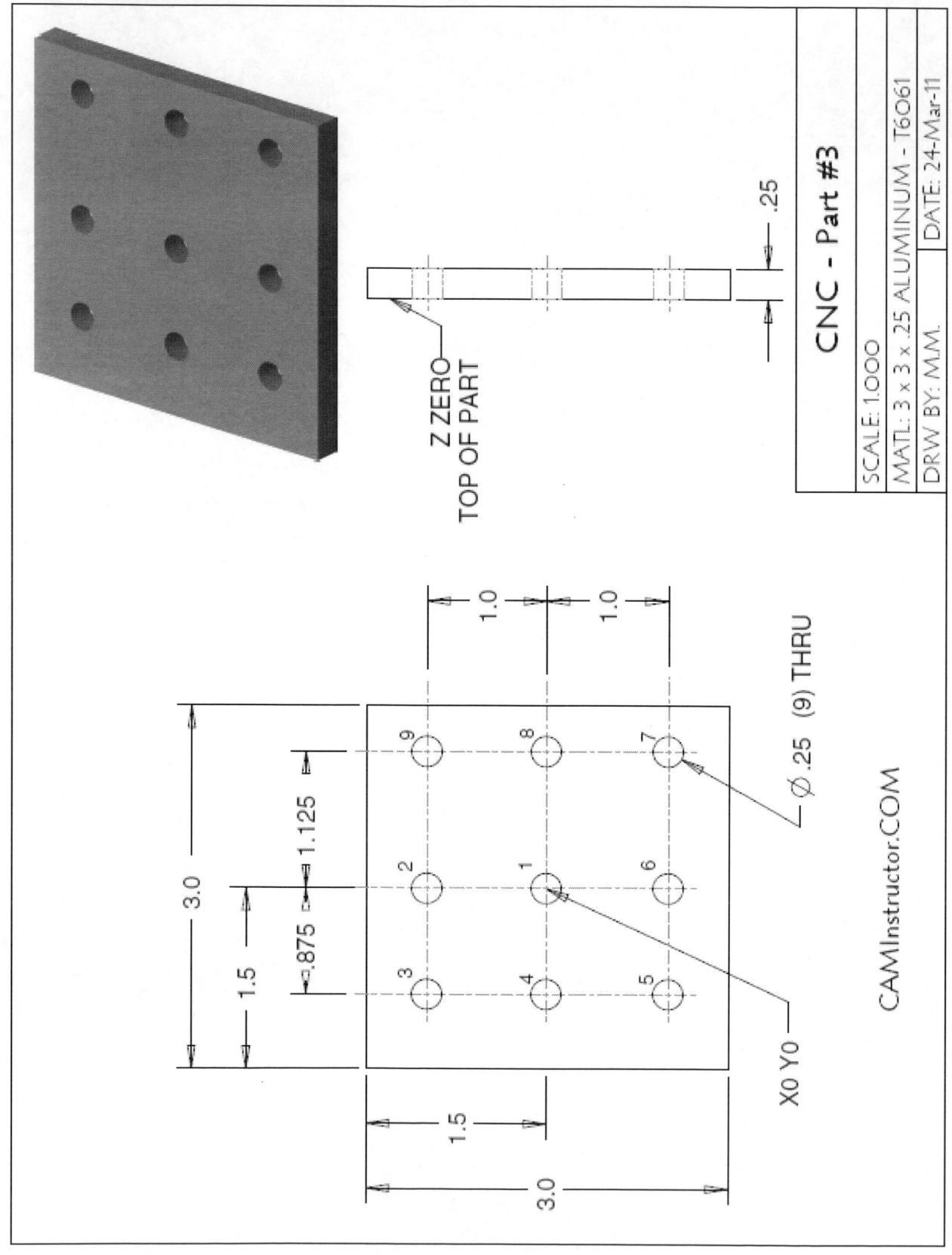

CNC - Part #3

SCALE: 1.000
MATL: 3 x 3 x .25 ALUMINUM - T6061
DRW BY: M.M.   DATE: 24-Mar-11

Z ZERO
TOP OF PART

Ø.25 (9) THRU

CAMInstructor.COM

X0 Y0

- ### *WORK OUT THE ABSOLUTE COORDINATES FOR THE NINE HOLES*
  - X0Y0 is at the centre of the part

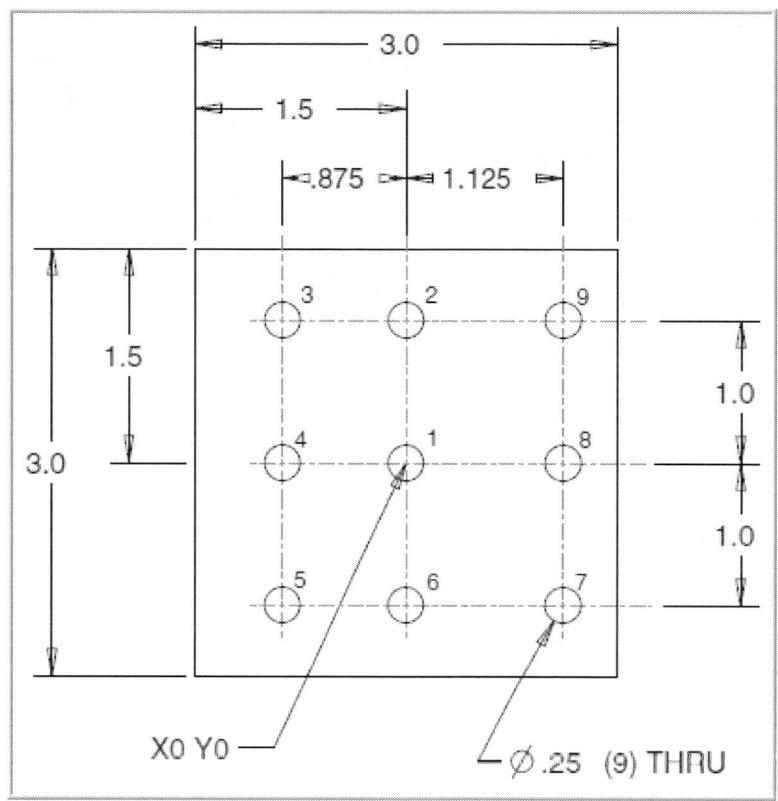

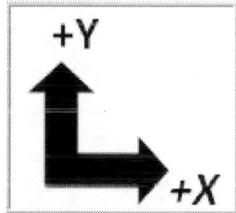

G90	X	Y
1		
2		
3		
4		
5		
6		
7		
8		
9		

LESSON-5 - CNC - PART #3

- ***CREATE THE PROGRAM TO <u>SPOT AND DRILL THE NINE HOLES</u> USING CANNED CYCLE G81***
    - Use a 0.375" diameter Spot Drill Tool # 6
    - Spot Drill Spindle Speed = 2750 Feed rate = 11 IPM
    - Use a 0.250" diameter Drill Tool # 7
    - 0.250" diameter Drill Spindle Speed = 4500 Feed rate = 15 IPM
    - Spot Drill Depth = Z-0.150"
    - Drill Depth = Z-0.350"
    - X0Y0 is at the centre of the part
    - Z=0 is the top of the part.
    - Type up your program and check it for correctness using the Backplot software.

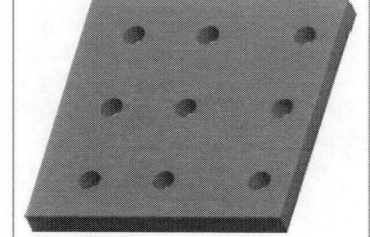

%
O5 (Program #5 - CNC-PART-3 - SPOT AND DRILLING USING CANNED CYCLE DRILL G81)
N10 G20
N20 G00 G17 G40 G49 G80 G90 (MACHINE DEFAULT SETTING)
N30

- ### *Use Discriminator to check for correctness*
  1. After typing up your program in Notepad launch the Discriminator application by clicking on the icon on your desktop or **Start>All Programs>Discriminator> Discriminator**

  2. Click **OK** to any warnings you receive.
  3. Click on **File>Open** and browse to your file location and select the CNC file to plot.

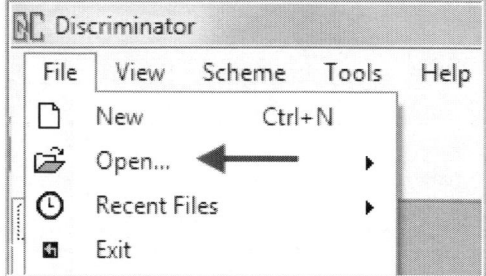

  4. After selecting the CNC file it opens up in a separate window.

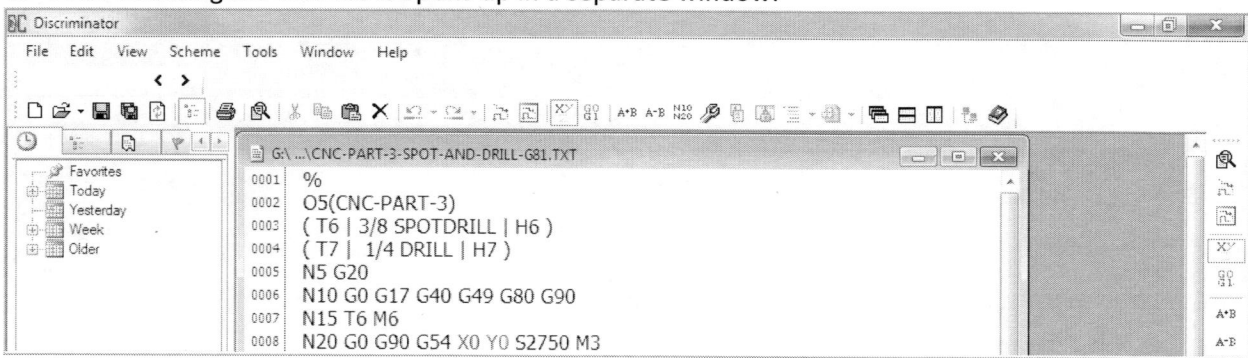

  5. Now click on the show graphics icon at the toolbar at the top of the screen to launch a plot of your CNC file.
  6. When the plot screen opens up hit the **Maximize** button and selects the icon to **View Fit**.
  7. You plot should appear as below. The point on the left of the screen shot below is the G53 X-15.0 Y0 movement in the program.

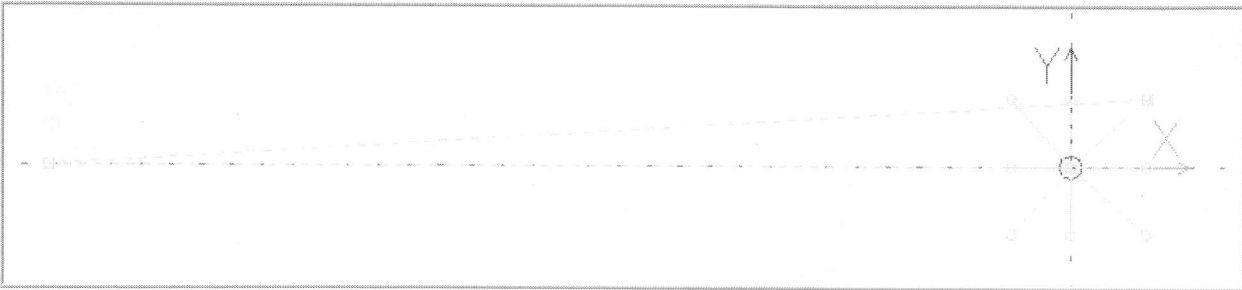

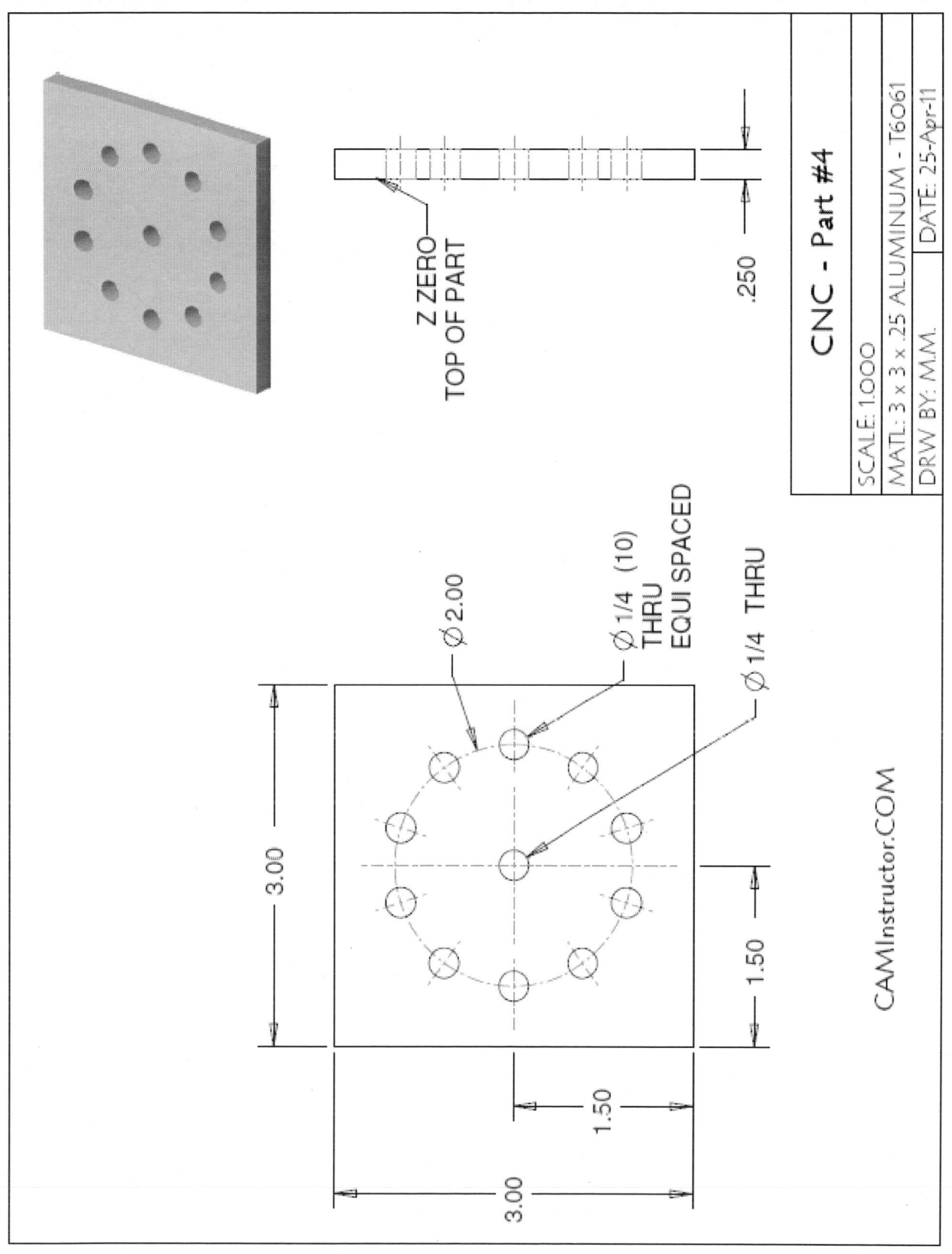

CNC - Part #4

SCALE: 1.000
MATL: 3 x 3 x .25 ALUMINUM - T6061
DRW BY: MM.   DATE: 25-Apr-11

Z ZERO
TOP OF PART

.250

Ø 2.00

Ø 1/4 (10)
THRU
EQUI SPACED

Ø 1/4 THRU

3.00

1.50

1.50

3.00

CAMInstructor.COM

- ## *WORK OUT THE ABSOLUTE COORDINATES FOR THE ELEVEN HOLES*
  - X0Y0 is at the centre of the part
  - Use Trigonometry to work out the center positions of the holes or draw the part up on a CAD system and then identify the center positions of each hole.

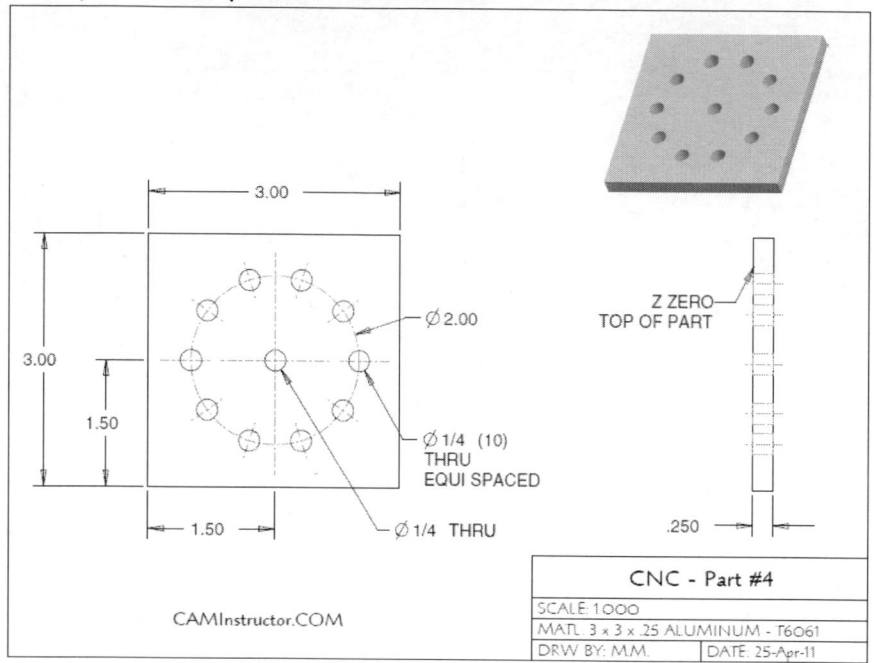

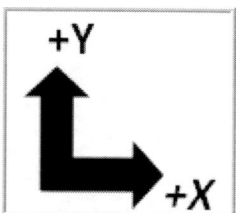

G90	X	Y
1	0	0
2		
3		
4		
5		
6		
7		
8		
9		
10		
11		

LESSON-5 - CNC - PART #4

- ***CREATE THE PROGRAM TO <u>SPOT AND DRILL THE ELEVEN HOLES</u> USING CANNED CYCLE G81***
  - Use a 0.375" diameter Spot Drill Tool # 6
  - Spot Drill Spindle Speed = 2750 Feed rate = 11 IPM
  - Use a 0.250" diameter Drill Tool # 7
  - 0.250" diameter Drill Spindle Speed = 4500 Feed rate = 15 IPM
  - Spot Drill Depth = Z-0.150"
  - Drill Depth = Z-0.350"
  - X0Y0 is at the centre of the part
  - Z=0 is the top of the part.
  - Type up your program and check it for correctness using the Backplot software.

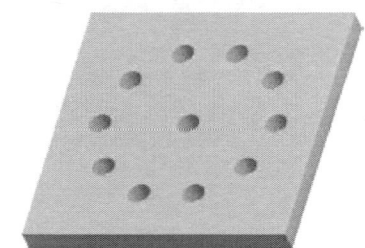

%
O99 (CNC-PART-4 - SPOT AND DRILLING USING CANNED CYCLE DRILL G81)
N10 G20
N20 G00 G17 G40 G49 G80 G90 (MACHINE DEFAULT SETTING)
N30

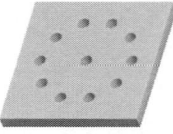

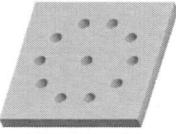

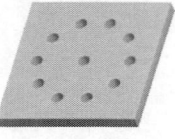

Mill Lesson 5 - 24

CNC Programming Workbook

+ Y

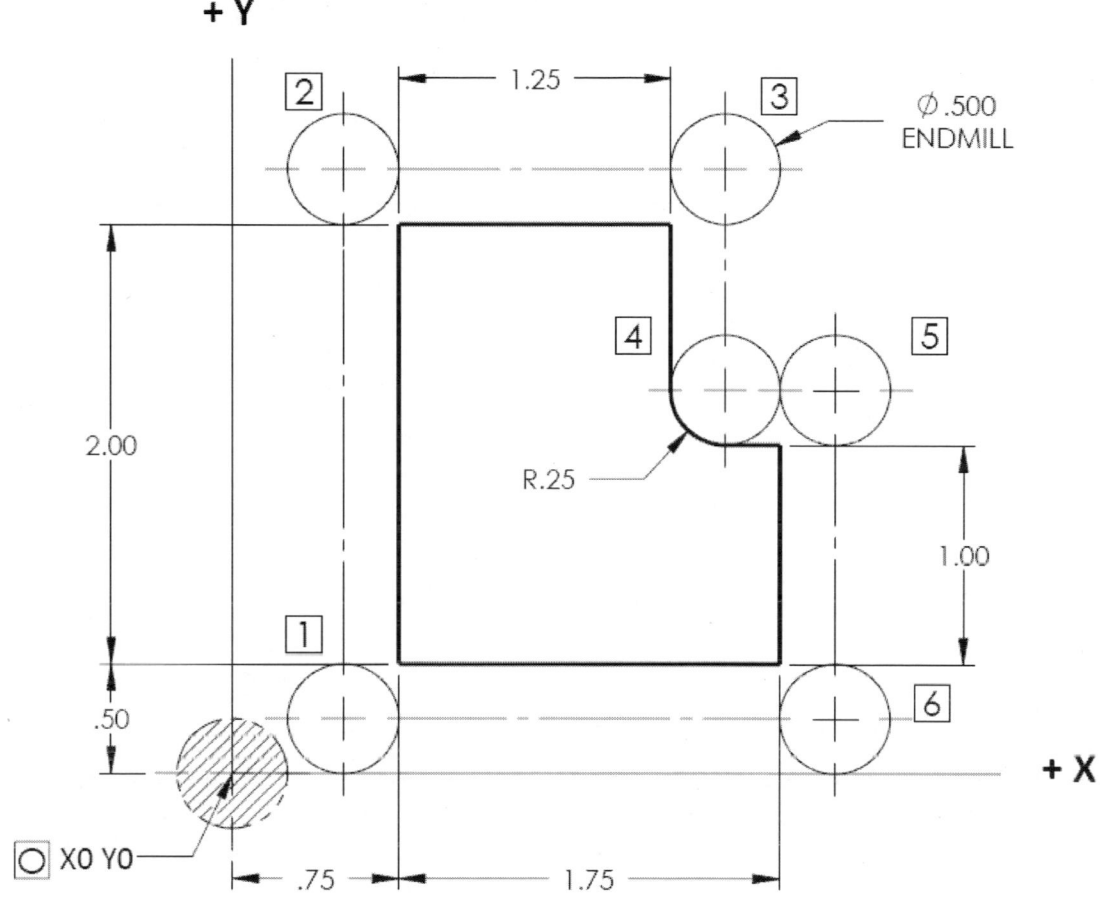

○ X0 Y0

+ X

Lesson-6

Straight Line Milling – Linear Interpolation

camInstructor

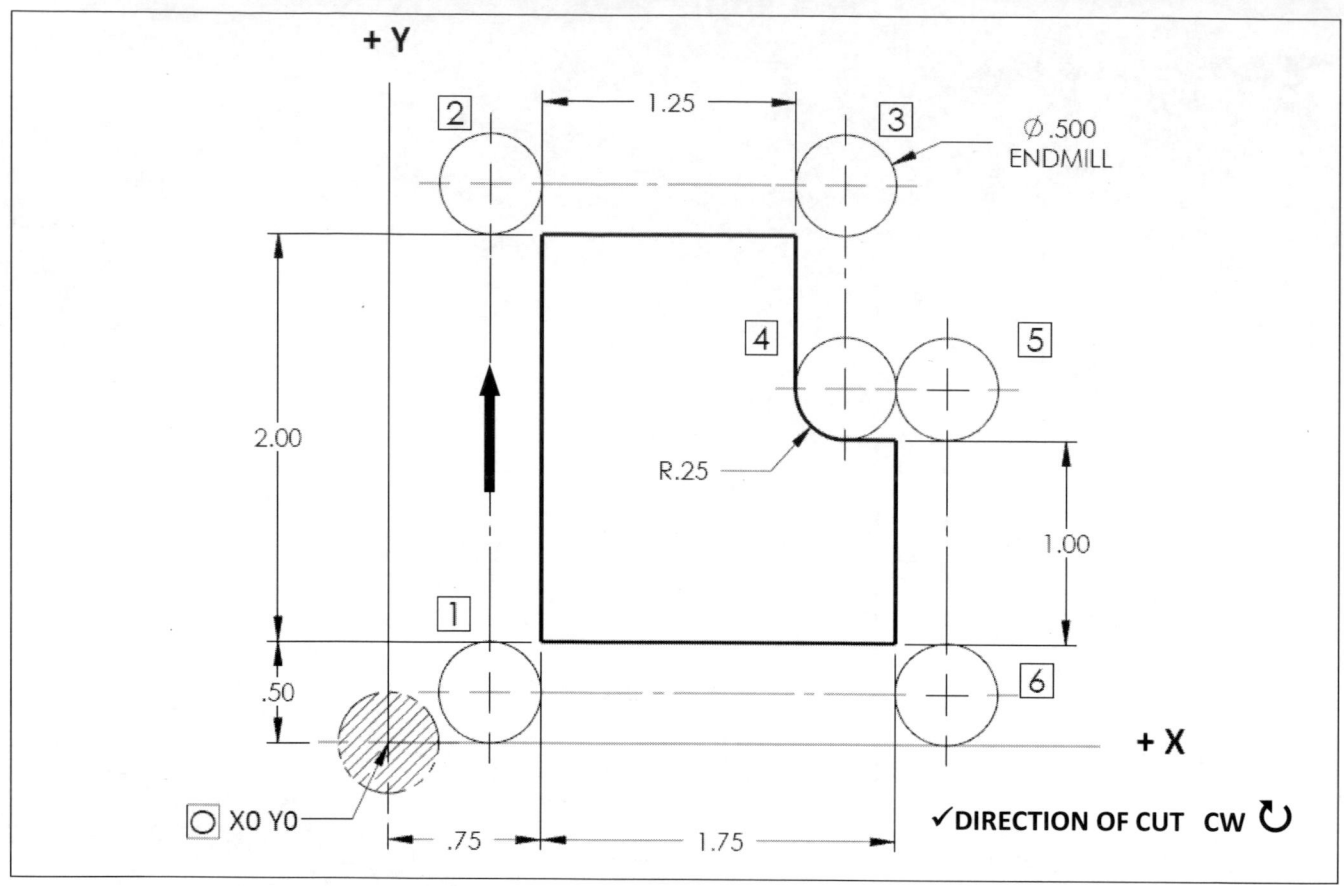

✏ **STARTING AT THE POINT O (ORIGIN), DESCRIBE THE ENDMILL PATH FROM O THROUGH ALL THE POINTS AND BACK TO THE POINT O USING G90 & G91. CUTTER DIAMETER = 0.5" RADIUS = 0.25'**

G90	X	Y	G91	X	Y
O	0	0	O → 1	0.5	0.25
1	0.5	0.25	1 → 2	0	2.5
2	0.5	2.75	2 → 3		
3			3 → 4		
4			4 → 5		
5			5 → 6		
6			6 → 1		
1			1 → O		
O					

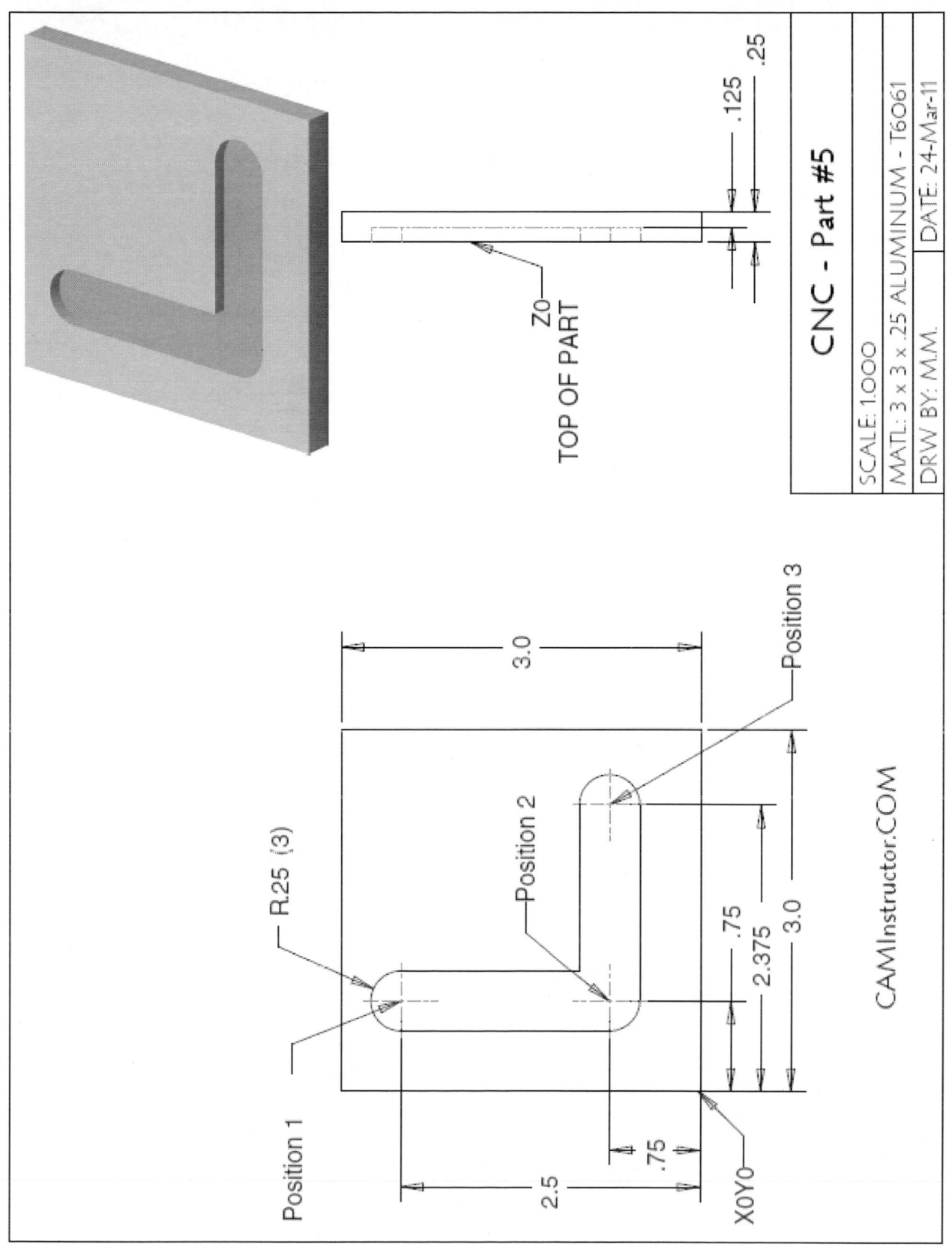

CNC - Part #5

.125

.25

Z0

TOP OF PART

SCALE: 1.000
MATL: 3 x 3 x .25 ALUMINUM - T6061
DRW BY: M.M.   DATE: 24-Mar-11

3.0

Position 3

Position 2

R25 (3)

.75

2.375

3.0

Position 1

.75

2.5

X0Y0

CAMInstructor.COM

- ### *WORK OUT THE ABSOLUTE COORDINATES FOR POSITION 1, 2 AND 3*
  - X0Y0 is at the lower left corner of the part
  - These X and Y coordinates will be used to machine the L shaped slot

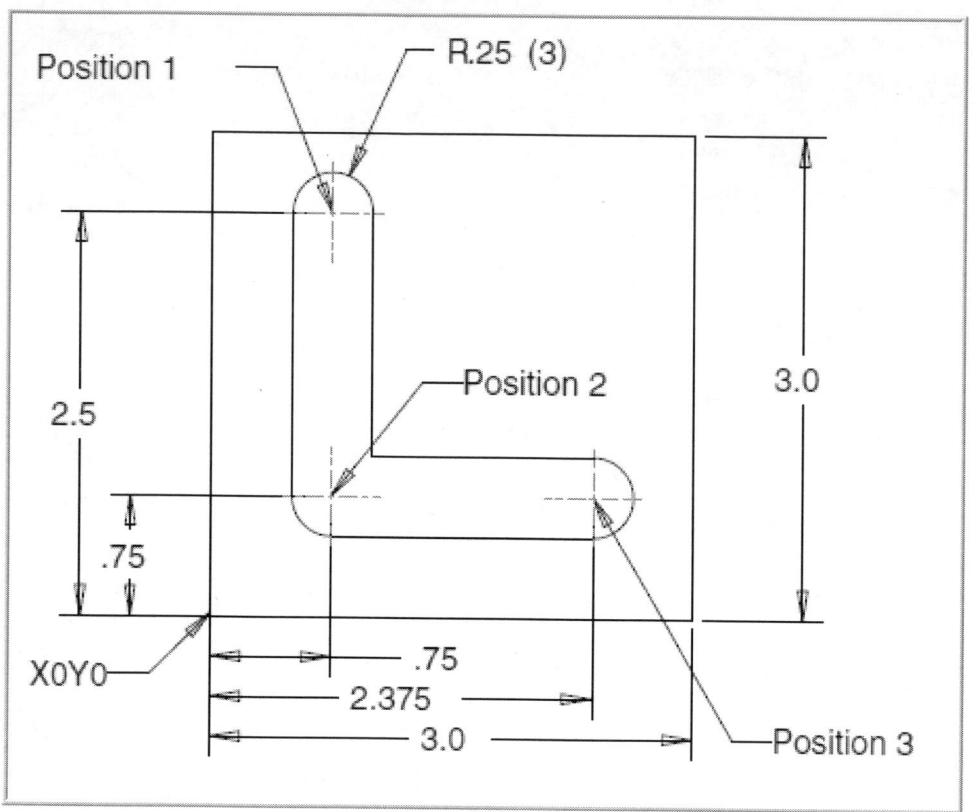

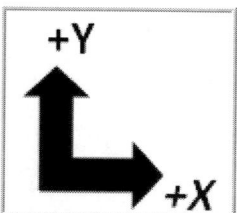

G90	X	Y
1		
2		
3		

- **PROGRAM TO MACHINE THE "L SHAPED" SLOT**
  - Use a 0.5" diameter End Mill Tool # 4
  - Speed = 3050 Feed rate =20 IPM
  - X0Y0 is at the lower left corner of the part
  - Z=0 is the top of the part.
  - The slot depth is 0.125"
  - Enter the part at Position 1 and sink to depth using linear interpolation G01
  - Then move to Position 2 and finally Position 3

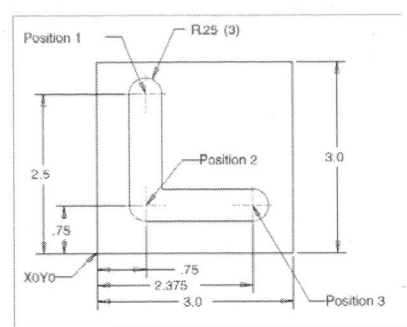

%	(Program must begin and end with a %)
O6	(Program #6 – Part #5 – STRAIGHT LINE MILLING)
(T4 - 1/2 FLAT ENDMILL - H4)	
N10 G20	**(Inch programming)**
N20 G00 G17 G40 G49 G80 G90 (MACHINE DEFAULT SETTING)	
N30 T4 M6	(T4-Select tool number 4 to be loaded M06-Activates the tool changer)
N40 G00 G90 G54 X0.75 Y2.5 S3050 M3 (Rapid to the X and Y to Position #1 and turn on the spindle at 3050 RPM)	
N50 G43 H04 Z0.1	(G43 - Activate the tool offset value stored in H04 and rapid to Z0.1)
N70 G1 Z-0.125 F10.	(Position #1 - Feed down to Z depth at 10 inches per minute)
N80 Y0.75 F20.0	(Move to Position #2 - at 20 inches per minute)
N90 X2.375	(Move to Position #3 - at 20 inches per minute)
N100 Z0.1 F10.0	(Retract out of the part at feedrate to 0.1 above the top of the work piece)
N120 M05	(Spindle off)
N130 G00 G91 G28 Z0	(G28 – Machine Zero positioning. Rapid to machine zero in Z)
N140 G28 X0 Y0	(G28 – Rapid in relation to machine zero X0 and Y0)
N150 G90	(RETURN TO ABSOLUTE PROGRAMMING)
N160 M30	(Program end rewind program to the beginning)
%	(Program must begin and end with a %)

In earlier programs we used **G53** to return the machine to coordinates in relation to the Machine Zero (home position). **G28** is another code that will accomplish this. **G28** is a more common way to send the machine to machine zero, it will work on many different types of CNC machines.

As you can see above at block **N130**, G28 is activated in **G91 incremental mode**, and then at block N150 the program is returned to **G90 absolute mode**.

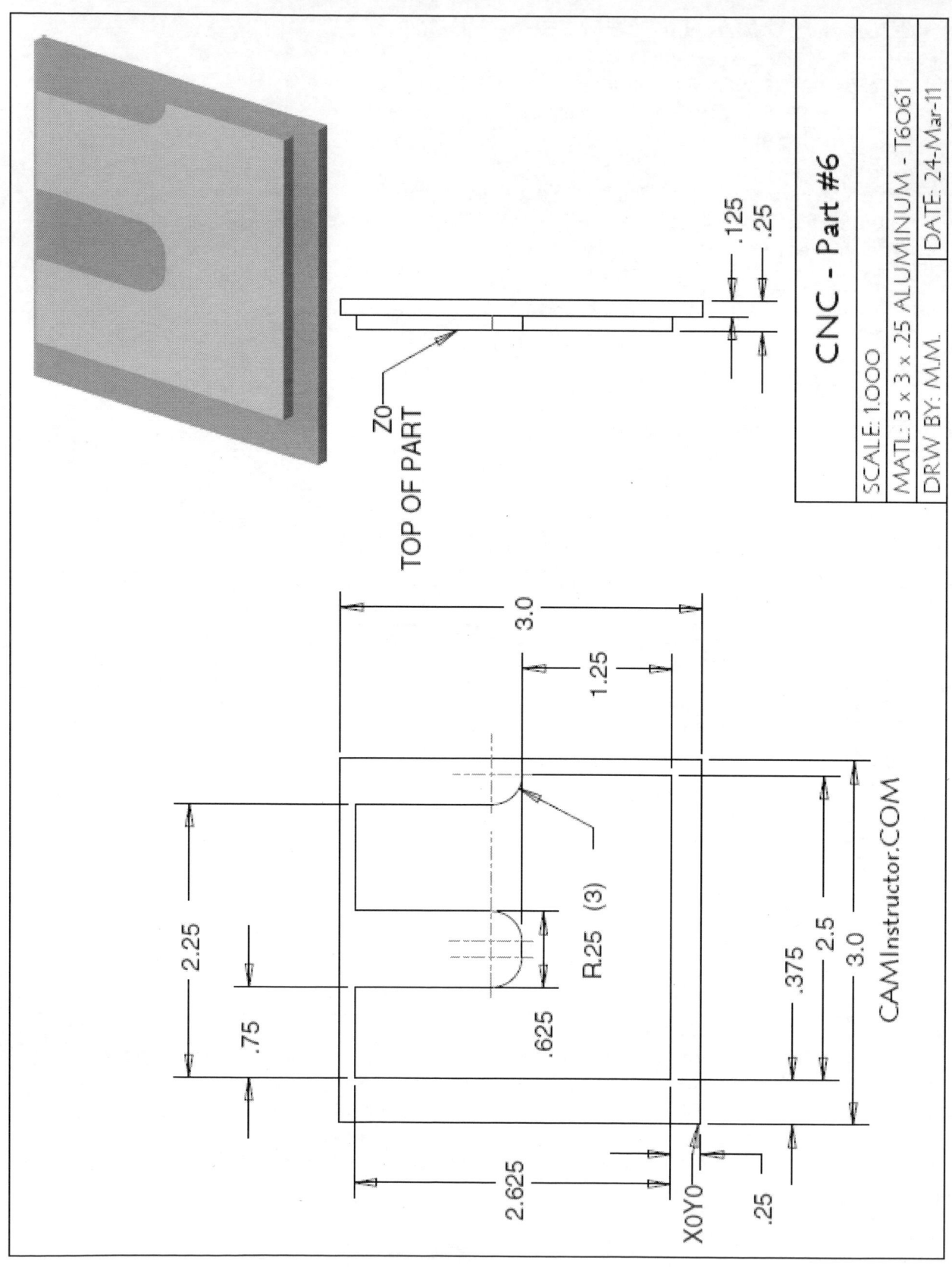

- ## *WORK OUT THE ABSOLUTE X AND Y COORDINATES FOR THE VARIOUS POSITIONS TO MACHINE THE CONTOUR*
  - X0Y0 is at the lower left corner of the part
  - Use a 0.5" diameter End Mill Tool # 4
  - Start at X-0.5 Y3.125 and machine the contour in a clockwise direction – climb milling

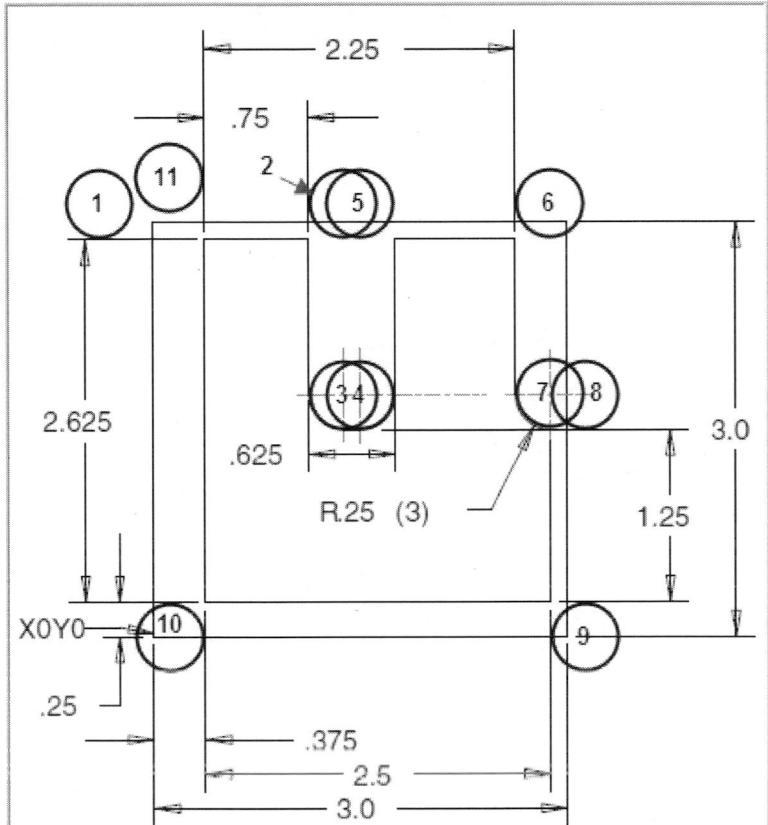

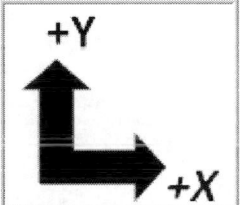

G90	X	Y
1	-0.5	3.125
2		
3		
4		
5		
6		
7		
8		
9		
10		
11		

- **PROGRAM TO MACHINE THE CONTOUR**
  - Use a 0.5" diameter End Mill Tool # 4
  - Speed = 3050 Feed rate =20 IPM
  - X0Y0 is at the lower left corner of the part
  - Z=0 is the top of the part.
  - Machine the contour at a depth is 0.125"

%	(Program must begin and end with a %)
O8	(Program #8 - CNC-PART-6 - STRAIGHT LINE MILLING)
(T4 - 1/2 FLAT ENDMILL - H4)	
N10 G20	**(Inch programming)**
N20 G00 G17 G40 G49 G80 G90 (MACHINE DEFAULT SETTING)	
N30 T4 M6	(T4-Select tool number 4 to be loaded M06-Activates the tool changer)
N40 G00 G90 G54 X-0.5 Y3. 125 S3050 M3	(Rapid to the X and Y to start Position #1 and turn on the spindle at 3050 RPM)
N50 G43 H04 Z0.1	(G43 - Activate the tool offset value stored in H04 and rapid to Z0.1)
N60 G1 Z-0.125 F10.	(Position #1 - Feed down to Z depth at 10 inches per minute)
N70 X1.375 F20.0	(Move to Position #2 - at 20 inches per minute)
N80 Y1.75	(Move to Position #3)
N90 X1.5	(Move to Position #4)
N100 Y3.125	(Move to Position #5)
N110 X2.875	(Move to Position #6)
N120 Y1.75	(Move to Position #7)
N130 X3.125	(Move to Position #8)
N140 Y0	(Move to Position #9)
N150 X0.125	(Move to Position #10)
N160 Y3.375	(Move to Position #11)
N170 Z0.1 F10.0	(Retract out of the part at feedrate to 0.1 above the top of the work piece)
N180 M05	(Spindle off)
N190 G00 G91 G28 Z0	(G28 – Machine Zero positioning. Rapid to machine zero in Z)
N200 G28 X0 Y0	(G28 – Rapid in relation to machine zero X0 and Y0)
N210 G90	(RETURN TO ABSOLUTE PROGRAMMING)
N220 M30	(Program end rewind program to the beginning)
%	(Program must begin and end with a %)

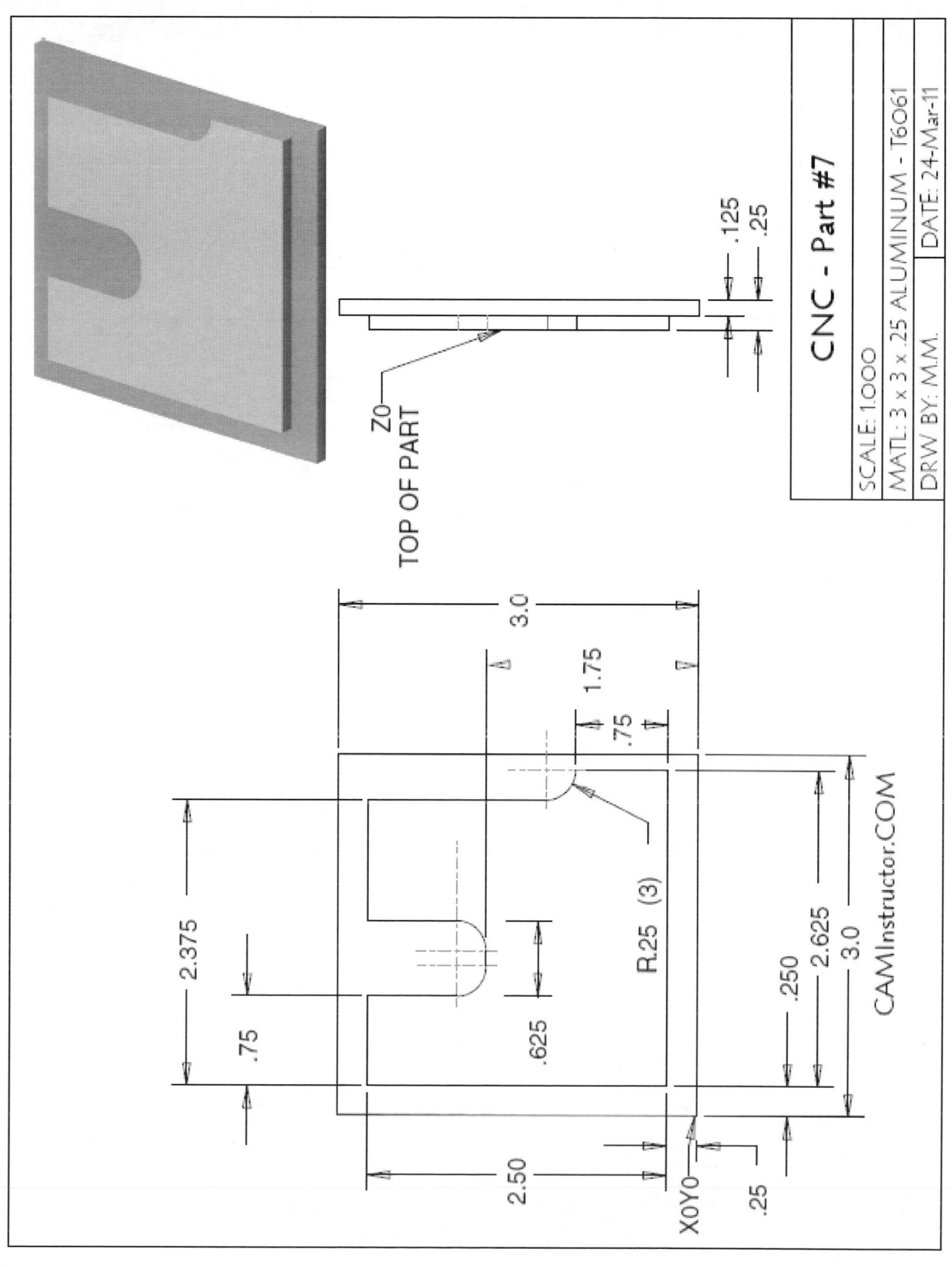

CNC - Part #7

SCALE: 1.000
MATL: 3 x 3 x .25 ALUMINUM - T6061
DRW BY: MM.   DATE: 24-Mar-11

.125
.25

Z0
TOP OF PART

3.0
1.75
.75
2.375
.75
R.25 (3)
.625
2.50
.250
2.625
3.0
X0Y0
.25

CAMInstructor.COM

- **WORK OUT THE ABSOLUTE X AND Y COORDINATES FOR THE VARIOUS POSITIONS TO MACHINE THE CONTOUR**
  - X0Y0 is at the lower left corner of the part
  - Use a 0.5" diameter End Mill Tool # 4
  - Start at X-0.5 Y3.0 and machine the contour in a clockwise direction – climb milling

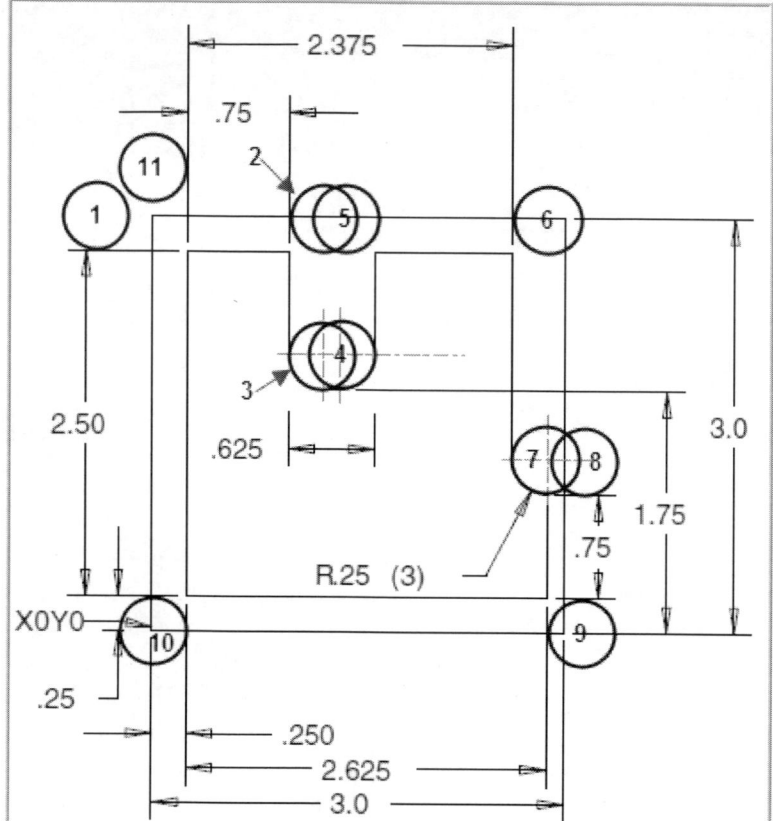

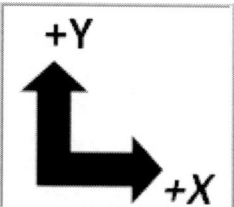

G90	X	Y
1	-0.5	3.0
2		
3		
4		
5		
6		
7		
8		
9		
10		
11		

- **CREATE THE PROGRAM TO MACHINE THE CONTOUR**
  - Use a 0.5" diameter End Mill Tool # 4
  - Speed = 3050 Feed rate =20 IPM
  - X0Y0 is at the lower left corner of the part
  - Z=0 is the top of the part.
  - Machine the contour at a depth is 0.125"
  - Start at X-0.5 Y3.0 and machine the contour in a clockwise direction – climb milling
  - Type up your program and check it for correctness using the Simulation software.

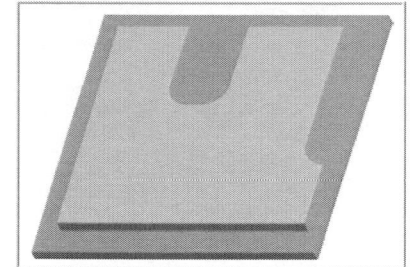

%	
O009	(Program #9 - CNC-PART-7 - STRAIGHT LINE MILLING)
N10 G20	
N20 G00 G17 G40 G49 G80 G90 (MACHINE DEFAULT SETTING)	
N30	

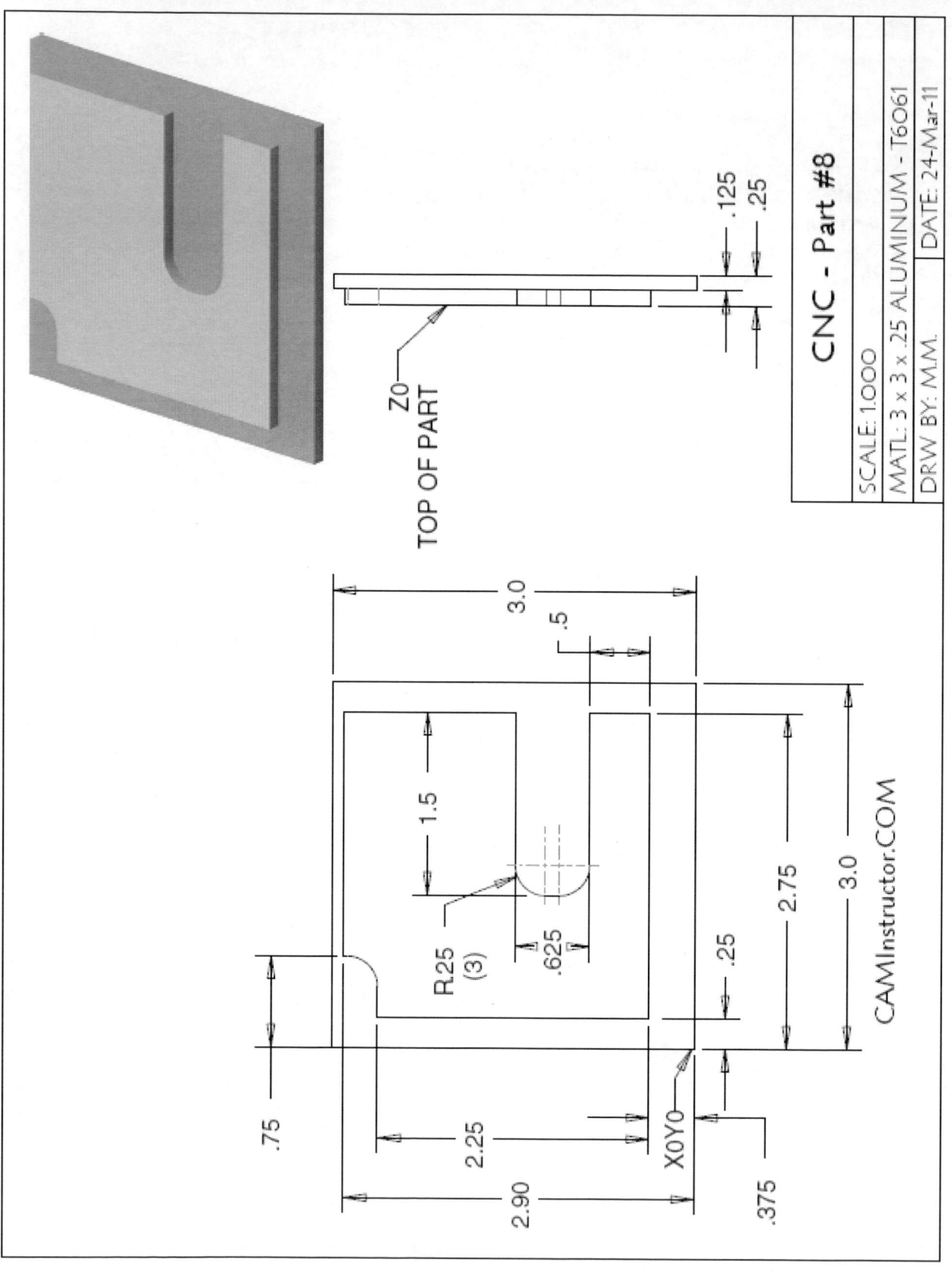

TOP OF PART

Z0

.125

.25

CNC - Part #8

SCALE: 1.000
MATL: 3 x 3 x .25 ALUMINUM - T6061
DRW BY: M.M.   DATE: 24-Mar-11

3.0

.5

1.5

R.25
(3)

.625

2.75

3.0

.25

.75

2.25

2.90

X0Y0

.375

CAMInstructor.COM

- **WORK OUT THE ABSOLUTE X AND Y COORDINATES FOR THE VARIOUS POSITIONS TO MACHINE THE CONTOUR**
  - X0Y0 is at the lower left corner of the part
  - Use a 0.5" diameter End Mill Tool # 4
  - Start at X0 Y-0.375 and machine the contour in a clockwise direction – climb milling

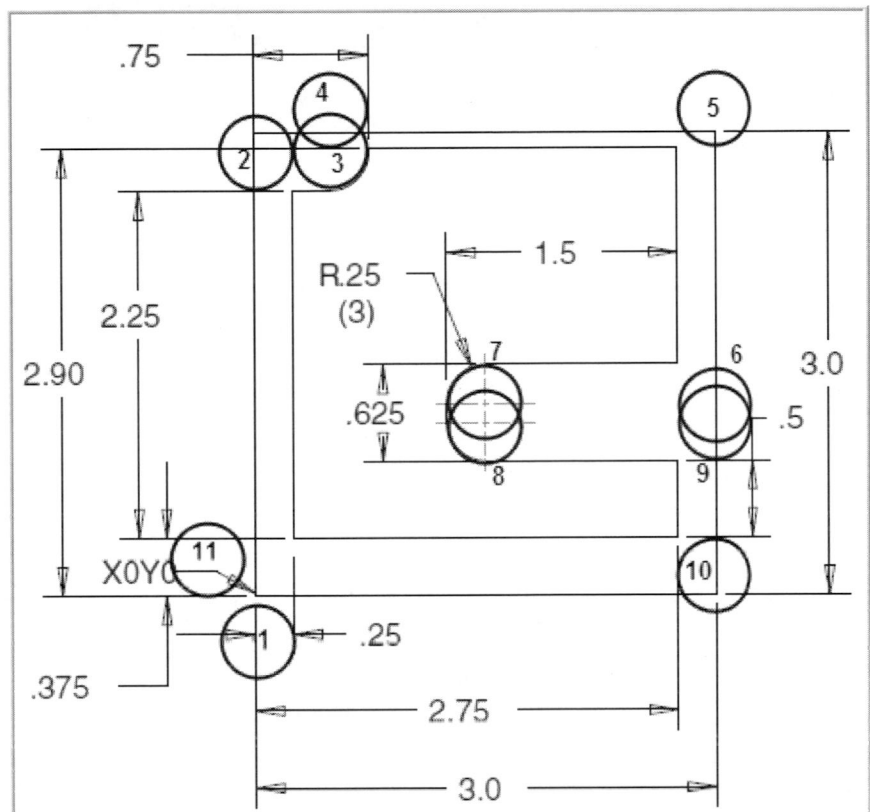

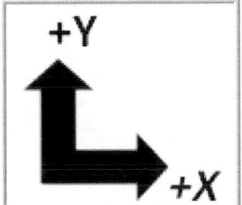

G90	X	Y
1	0	-0.375
2		
3		
4		
5		
6		
7		
8		
9		
10		
11		

- **CREATE THE PROGRAM TO MACHINE THE CONTOUR**
  - Use a 0.5" diameter End Mill Tool # 4
  - Speed = 3050 Feed rate =20 IPM
  - X0Y0 is at the lower left corner of the part
  - Z=0 is the top of the part.
  - Machine the contour at a depth is 0.125"
  - Start at X-0.5 Y3.0 and machine the contour in a clockwise direction – climb milling
  - Type up your program and check it for correctness using the Simulation software.

%	
O10	(Program #10 - CNC-PART- 8 - STRAIGHT LINE MILLING)
N10	G20
N20	G00 G17 G40 G49 G80 G90 (MACHINE DEFAULT SETTING)
N30	

CNC PROGRAMMING
WORKBOOK

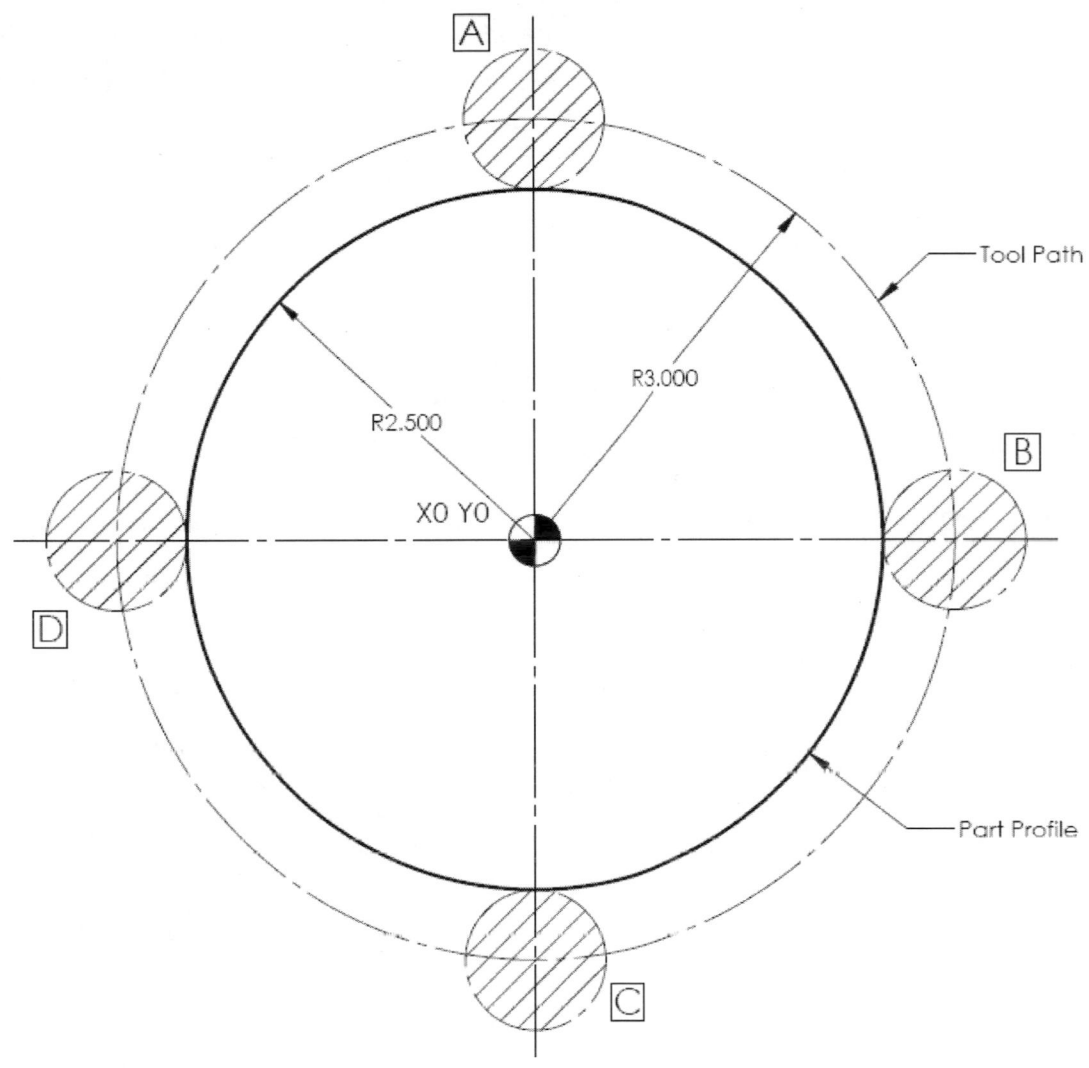

LESSON-7

CIRCULAR INTERPOLATION

camInstructor

- *In the next series of circular interpolation exercises you will explore how to machine arcs and complete circles.*
- *G02 and G03 allow the machining of circles and arcs*

When the machine is required to move in a straight line under a controlled federate, linear interpolation is used G01. When it is necessary to machine in a circular motion in any plane (XY, YZ, XZ) circular interpolation is used G02 and G03.

All circular interpolation moves are defined using three pieces of information.

1. *DIRECTION OF TRAVEL: CLOCKWISE G02, COUNTER CLOCKWISE G03*

2. *PROGRAMMED END POINT OF THE ARC*

3. *ARC CENTER: INCREMENTAL DISTANCE FROM START POINT TO ARC CENTER (I, J, K OR R FOR RADIUS, I,J AND K ARE NOT USED)*

- *When trying to figure out a circular interpolation move answer these three questions:*
  - I.   What is the direction of travel, clockwise or counterclockwise – G02 or G03?
  - II.   Where is the programmed end point?
  - III. What is the incremental distance from the start of the arc to the center of the arc being machined – I and J values?

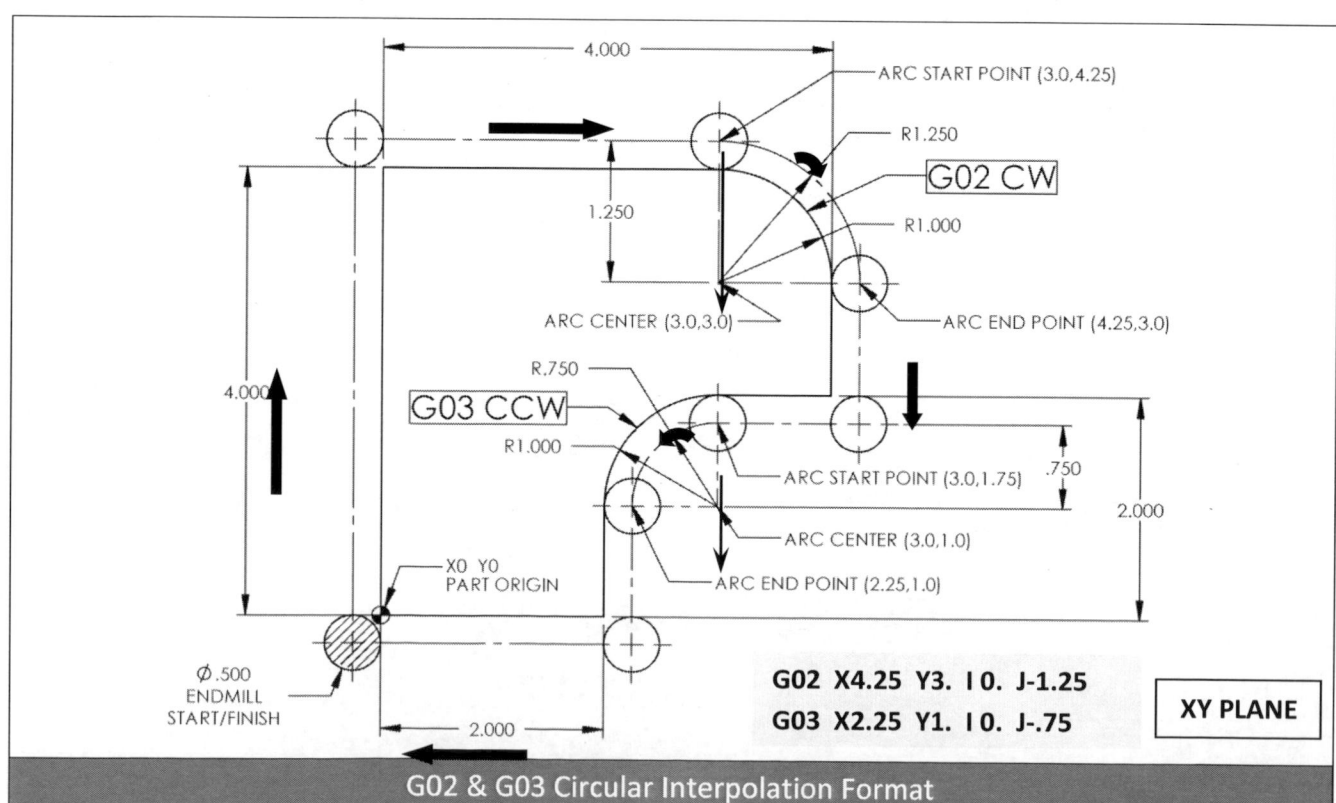

G02 & G03 Circular Interpolation Format

G02 -Clockwise or G03 Counter Clockwise?

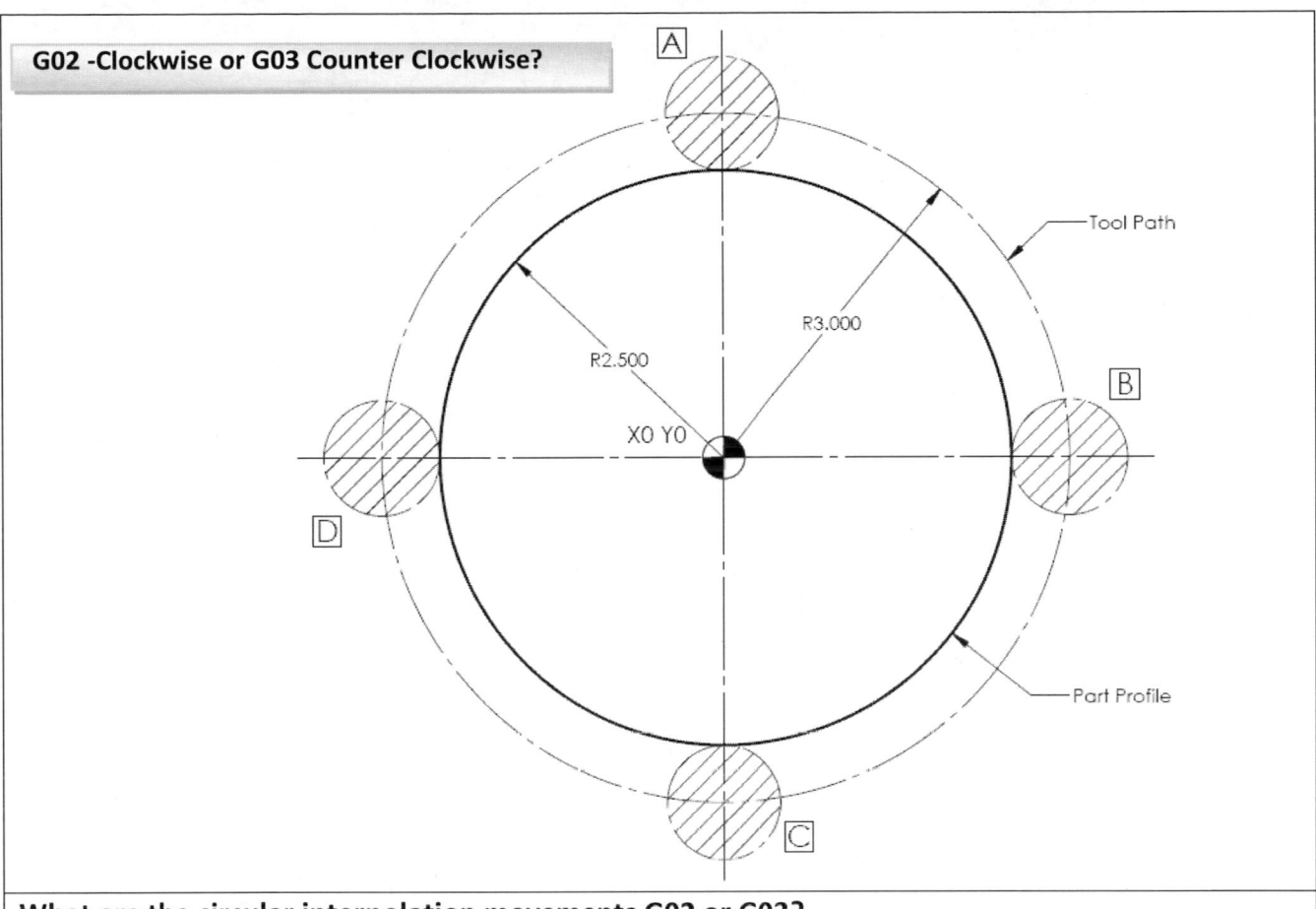

What are the circular interpolation movements G02 or G03?

1. A to B Circular Interpolation (CW) **G02**

2. A to C Circular Interpolation (CW) **G02**

3. D to C Circular Interpolation (CCW) ?

4. D to B Circular Interpolation (CCW) ?

5. A to A Circular Interpolation (CW) ?

1.0" Diameter End Mill

Radius = 0.5

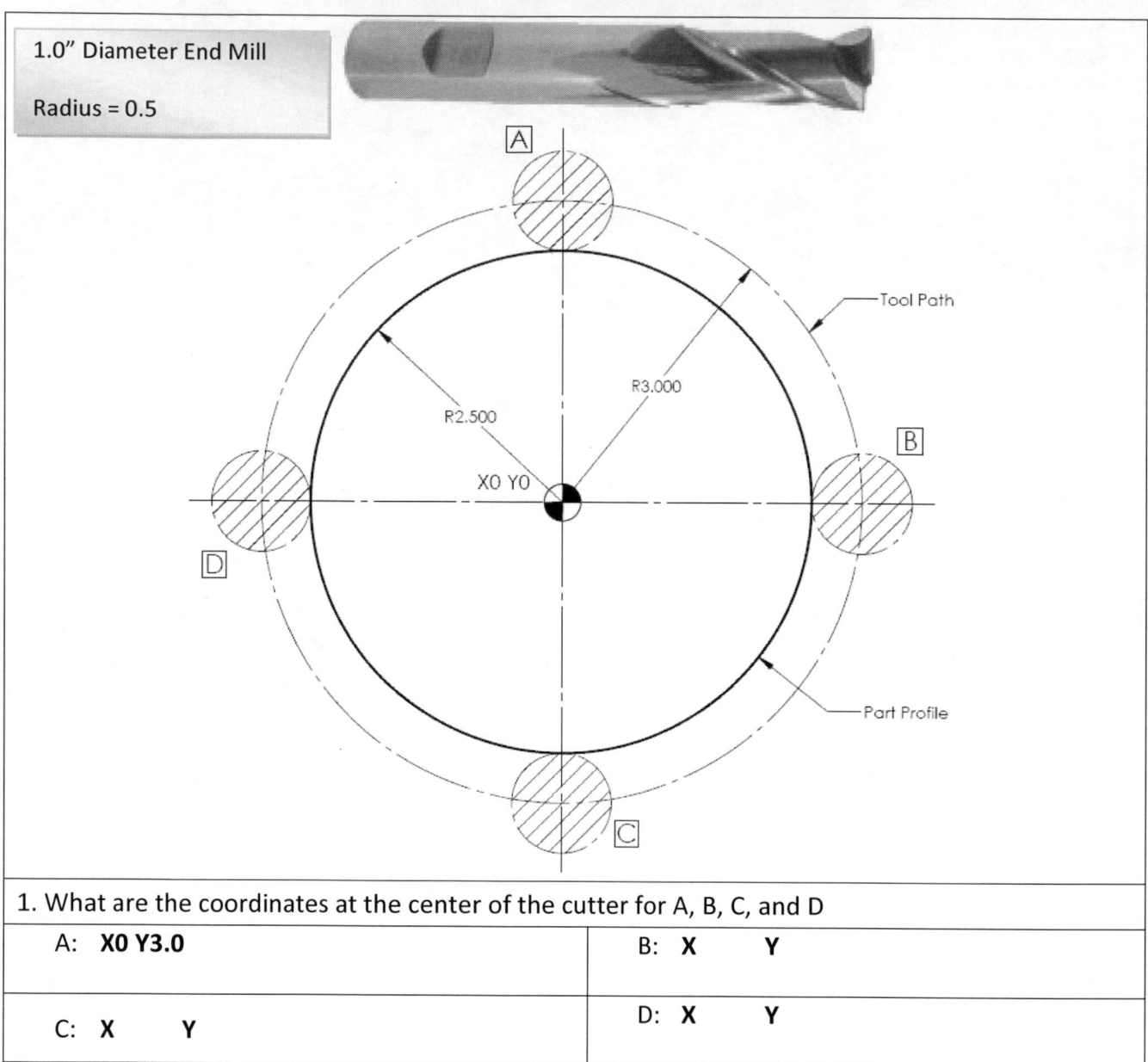

1. What are the coordinates at the center of the cutter for A, B, C, and D

A: **X0 Y3.0**	B: **X** **Y**
C: **X** **Y**	D: **X** **Y**

- ***I , J and K Values are measured from the tool start to the center of the arc***
- ***I , J and K values are INCREMENTAL***
- ***I= X Axis   J = Y Axis   K= Z Axis***

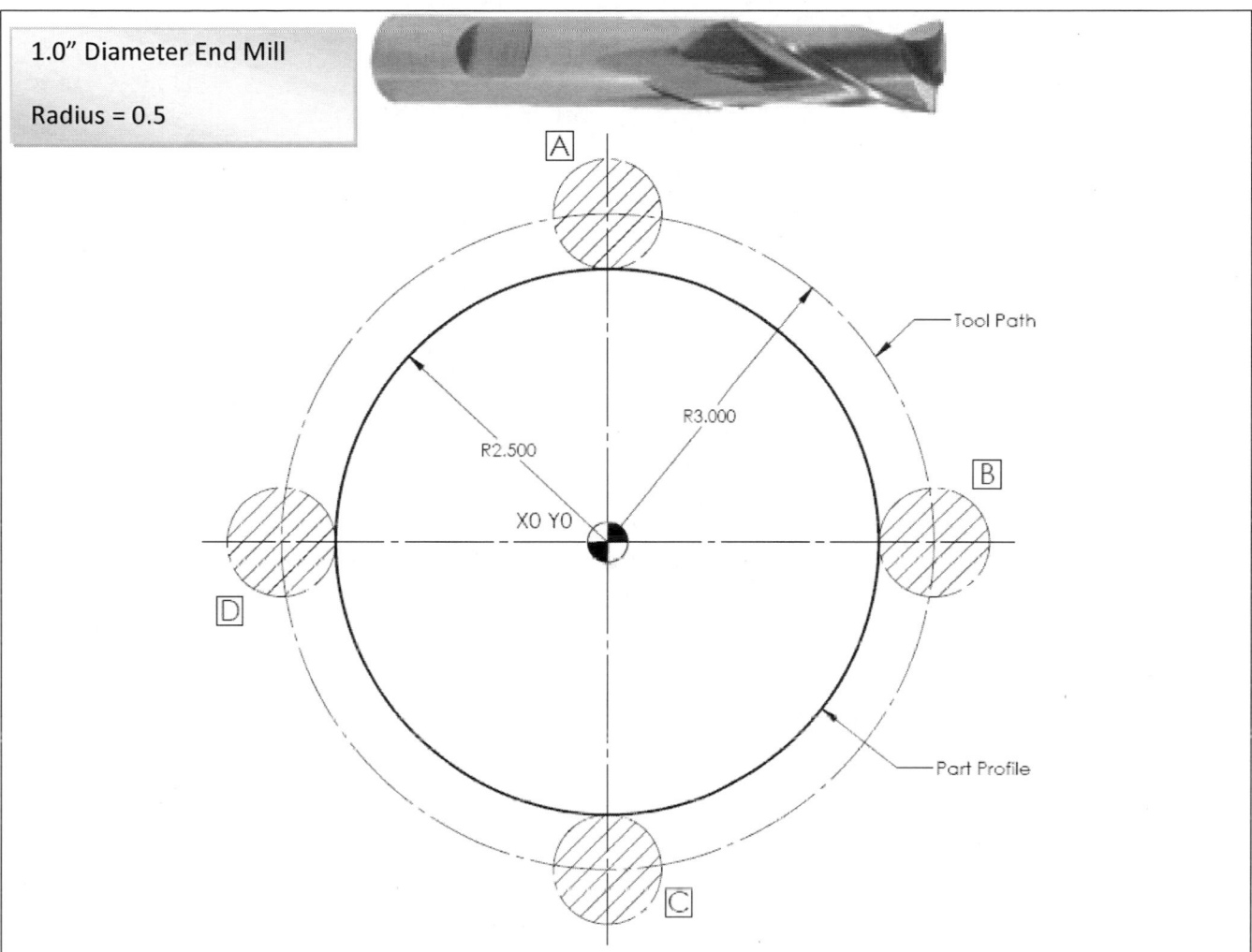

1.0" Diameter End Mill

Radius = 0.5

R3.000

R2.500

X0 Y0

Tool Path

Part Profile

A B C D

1. What are the **incremental** distances from the start of cut to the center of the programmed arc?
   - I = The Incremental distance along the **X axis** from the start of the arc to the center of the programmed arc
   - J = The Incremental distance along the **Y axis** from the start of the arc to the center of the programmed arc

A to the centre of the circle: **I0 J-3.0**	B to the centre of the circle: **I J**
C to the centre of the circle: **I J**	D to the centre of the circle: **I J**

- *What does the block of code look like moving from D to B clockwise?*
  - *G02 X3.0 Y0 I3.0 J0*
- *What does the block of code look like moving from A to D counterclockwise?*
  - *G03 X-3.0 Y0 I-3.0 J0*

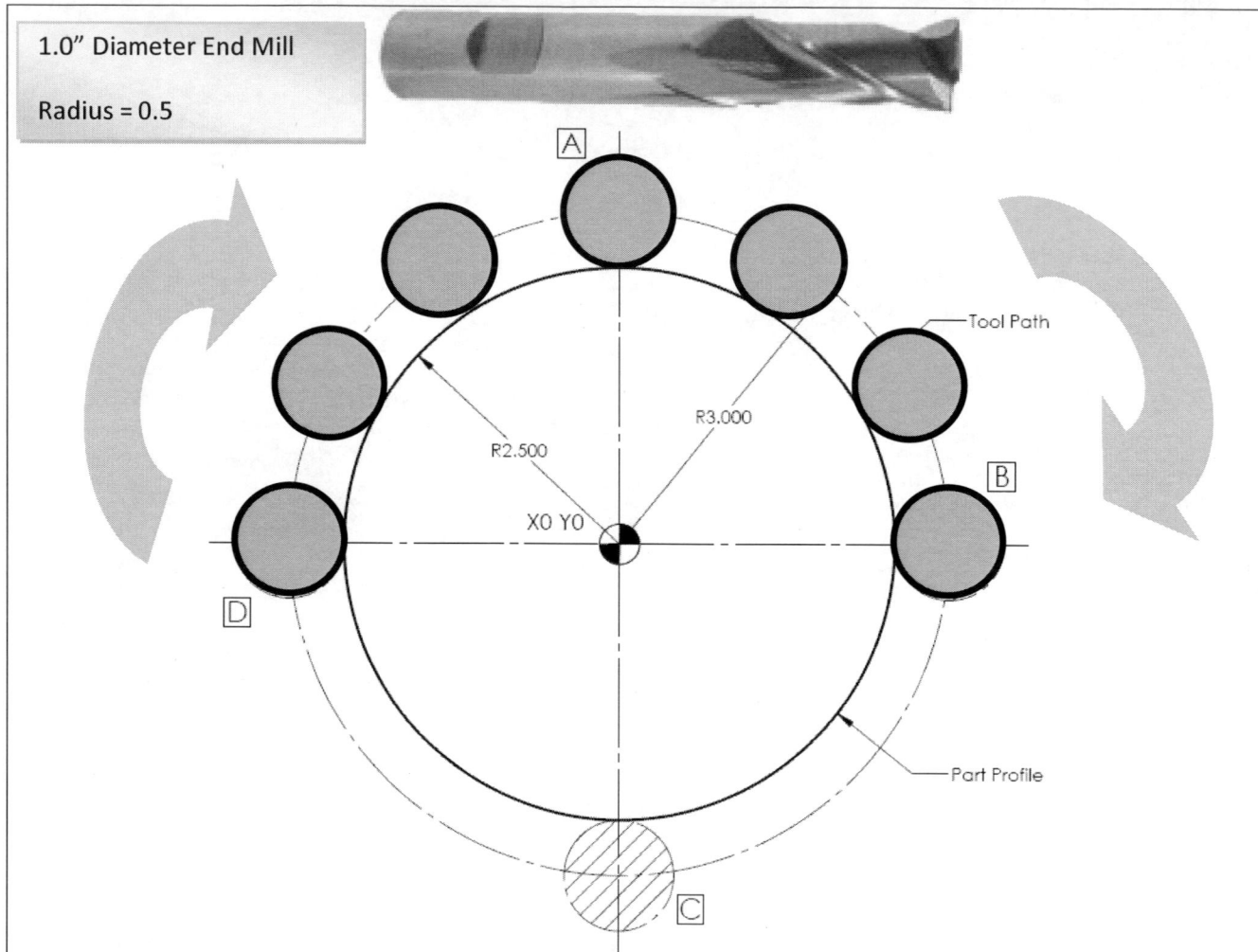

- *When trying to figure out a circular interpolation move answer these three questions:*
  I. What is the direction of travel, clockwise or counterclockwise – G02 or G03?
  II. Where is the programmed end point?
  III. What is the incremental distance from the start of the arc to the center of the arc being machined – I and J values?
- *Work out the following circular interpolation blocks*

C to D Clockwise:	**D to C** Counterclockwise:
A to A Clockwise:	**B to C** Counterclockwise:

- *The center of the circle has now been changed to X5.0 Y5.0*
- *What does the block of code look like moving from D to B clockwise?*
  - *G02 X8.0 Y5.0 I3.0 J0*
- *What does the block of code look like moving from A to D counterclockwise?*
  - *G03 X2.0 Y5.0 I-3.0 J0*

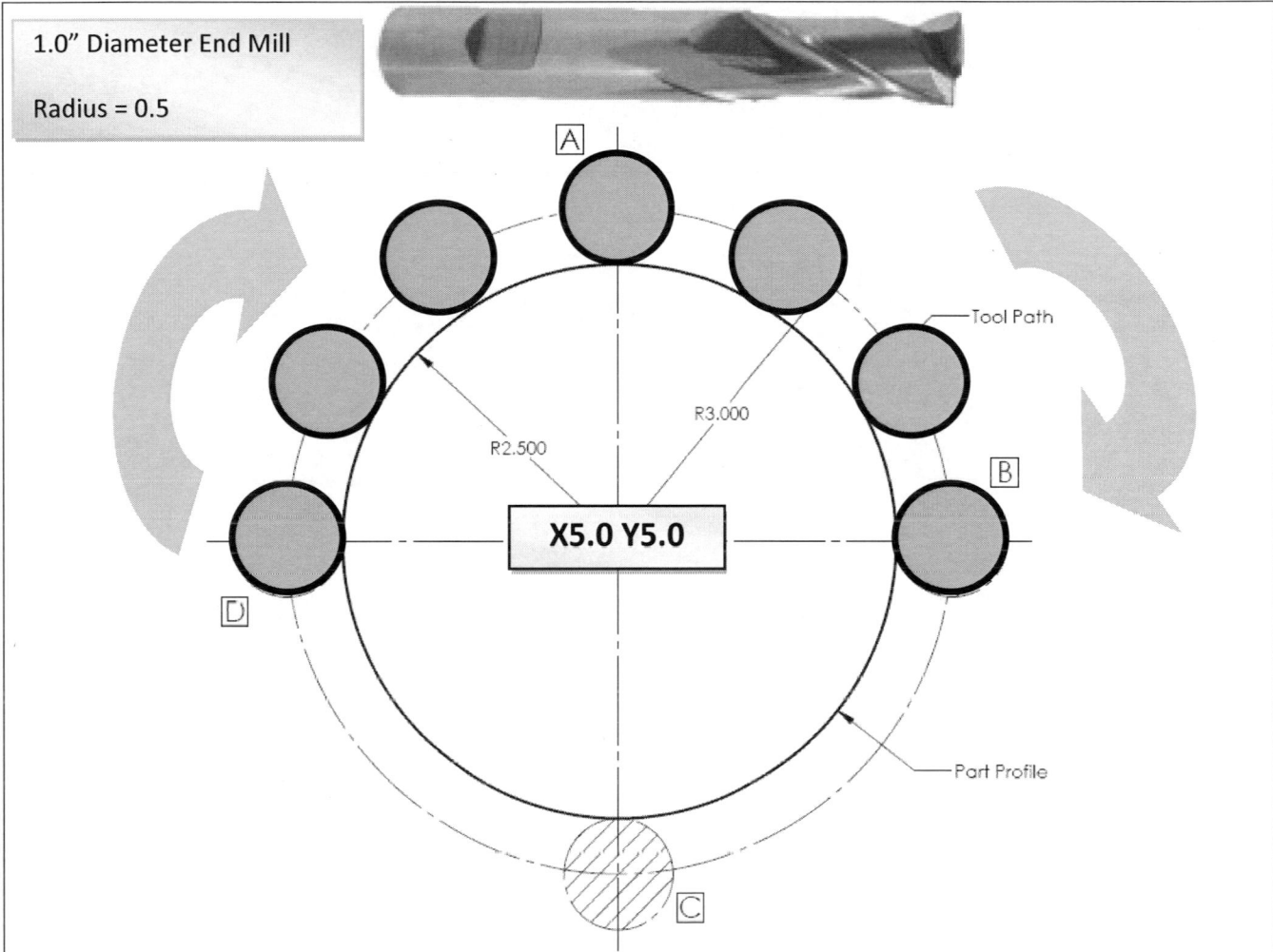

1.0" Diameter End Mill

Radius = 0.5

R3.000

R2.500

X5.0 Y5.0

Tool Path

Part Profile

- *When trying to figure out a circular interpolation move answer these three questions:*
  - I. What is the direction of travel, clockwise or counterclockwise – G02 or G03?
  - II. Where is the programmed end point?
  - III. What is the incremental distance from the start of the arc to the center of the arc being machined – I and J values?
- *Work out the following circular interpolation blocks*

C to D Clockwise:	**D to C** Counterclockwise:
A to A Clockwise:	**B to C** Counterclockwise:

To cut a complete circle of 360°, you do not need to specify an end point X, Y, or Z. Just program I, J, or K to define the centre of the circle.

Work out the following circular interpolation blocks

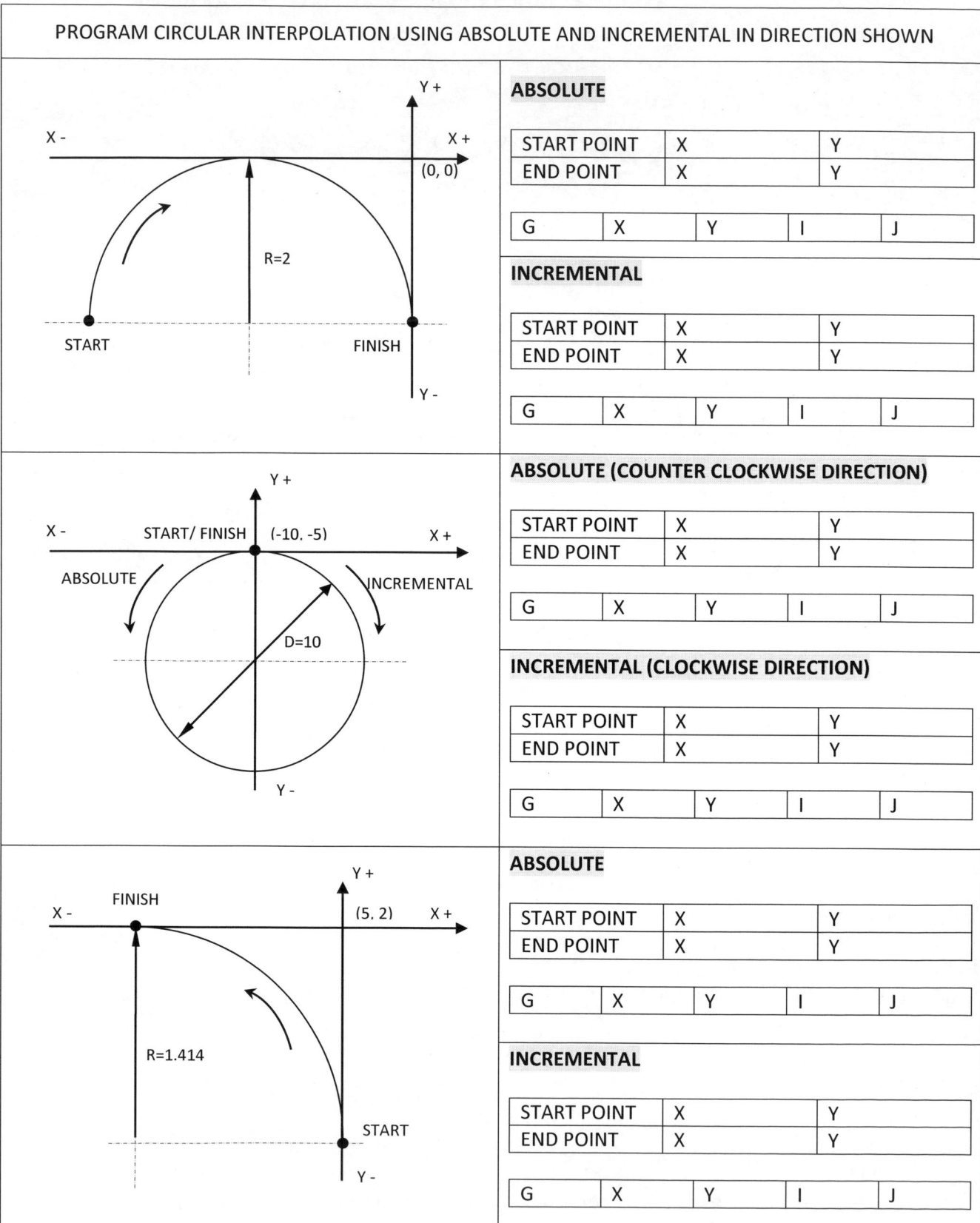

PROGRAM CIRCULAR INTERPOLATION USING ABSOLUTE AND INCREMENTAL IN DIRECTION SHOWN

ABSOLUTE

START POINT	X		Y	
END POINT	X		Y	

G	X	Y	I	J

INCREMENTAL

START POINT	X		Y	
END POINT	X		Y	

G	X	Y	I	J

ABSOLUTE (COUNTER CLOCKWISE DIRECTION)

START POINT	X		Y	
END POINT	X		Y	

G	X	Y	I	J

INCREMENTAL (CLOCKWISE DIRECTION)

START POINT	X		Y	
END POINT	X		Y	

G	X	Y	I	J

ABSOLUTE

START POINT	X		Y	
END POINT	X		Y	

G	X	Y	I	J

INCREMENTAL

START POINT	X		Y	
END POINT	X		Y	

G	X	Y	I	J

Review the CNC program below that machines the contour.

- The cutter being used is a 0.5" diameter end mill.
- X0 Y0 is the lower left corner of the part.
- Start position lower left corner, machines clockwise.
- The blocks of CNC code are made up of G01 and a G02 moves.
- Note that the G02 move to machine the 0.5" and 0.25" radius can use either **I and J** values or **R** for the radius.

All circular interpolation moves are defined using three pieces of information.

1. *DIRECTION OF TRAVEL: CLOCKWISE G02, COUNTER CLOCKWISE G03*

2. *ARC END POINT*

3. *ARC CENTER: INCREMENTAL DISTANCE FROM START POINT TO ARC CENTER (I, J, K)*

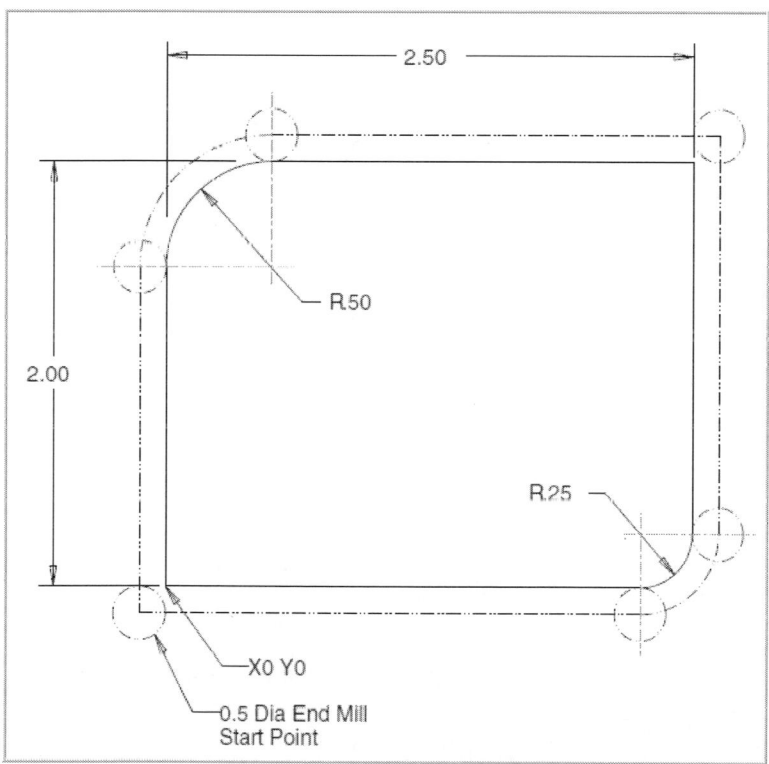

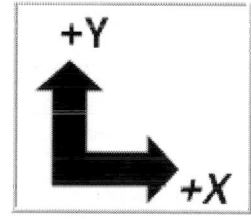

N160 G1 X-.25 Y-.25 (start position)	I = The Incremental distance along the **X axis** from the start of the arc to the center of the programmed arc
N170 Y1.5	
N180 G2 X.5 Y2.25 I.75 J0. (OR R0.5)	
N190 G1 X2.75	
N200 Y.25	J = The Incremental distance along the **Y axis** from the start of the arc to the center of the programmed arc
N210 G2 X2.25 Y-.25 I-.5 J0. (OR R0.25)	
N220 G1 X-.25	

Review the CNC program below that machines the contour.

- The cutter being used is a 0.5" diameter end mill.
- X0 Y0 is the center of the part.
- Start position is the upper right, machines clockwise.
- The blocks of CNC code are made up of G01 and a G02 moves.
- Note that the G02 move to machine the radii can use either **I and J** values or **R** for the radius.

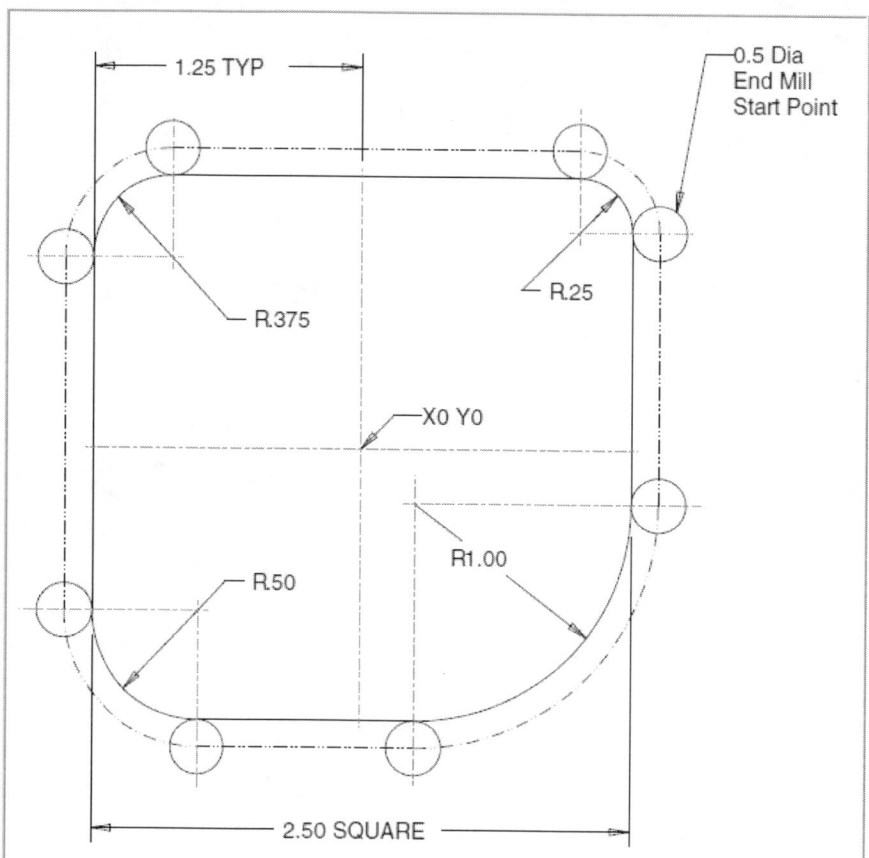
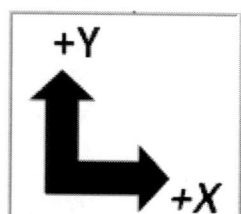

Using I and J Values	Using R for Radius Values
N160 G1 X1.5 Y1.0 (start position)	**N160 G1 X1.5 Y1.0 (start position)**
N170 Y-.25	**N170 Y-.25**
N180 G2 X.25 Y-1.5 I-1.25 J0.	**N180 G2 X.25 Y-1.5 R1.25**
N190 G1 X-.75	**N190 G1 X-.75**
N200 G2 X-1.5 Y-.75 I0. J.75	**N200 G2 X-1.5 Y-.75 R.75**
N210 G1 Y.875	**N210 G1 Y.875**
N220 G2 X-.875 Y1.5 I.625 J0.	**N220 G2 X-.875 Y1.5 R.625**
N230 G1 X1.	**N230 G1 X1.**
N240 G2 X1.5 Y1. I0. J-.5	**N240 G2 X1.5 Y1. R.5**

To cut a complete circle of 360°, you do not need to specify an end point X, Y, or Z. Just program I, J, or K to define the centre of the circle.

Review the CNC program below that machines the contour around the inside of the pocket.

- The cutter being used is a 0.5" diameter end mill.
- X0 Y0 is the center of the part.
- Start position is the upper right, machines contour counter clockwise.
- The blocks of CNC code are made up of G01 and a G03 moves.
- Note that the G03 move to machine the radii can use either **I and J** values or **R** for the radius.

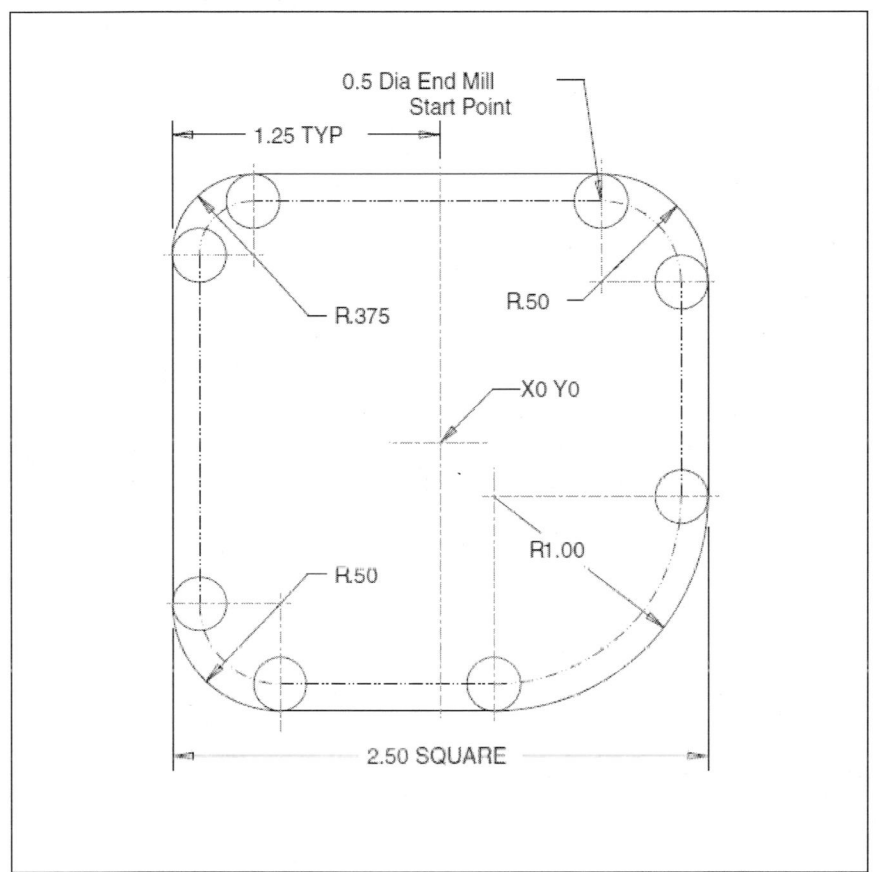

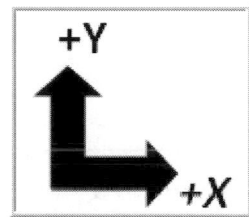

Using I and J Values	Using R for Radius Values
N40 G0 G90 G54 X.75 Y1. A0. S2500 M3	N40 G0 G90 G54 X.75 Y1. A0. S2500 M3
N50 G43 H4 Z.35	N50 G43 H4 Z.35
N60 G1 Z.125 F15.	N60 G1 Z.125 F15.
N70 X-.875	N70 X-.875
N80 G3 X-1. Y.875 I0. J-.125 (0.375 Radius)	N80 G3 X-1. Y.875 R.125 (0.375 Radius)
N90 G1 Y-.75	N90 G1 Y-.75
N100 G3 X-.75 Y-1. I.25 J0. (0.5 Radius)	N100 G3 X-.75 Y-1. R.25 (0.5 Radius)
N110 G1 X.25	N110 G1 X.25
N120 G3 X1. Y-.25 I0. J.75 (1.0 Radius)	N120 G3 X1. Y-.25 R.75 (1.0 Radius)
N130 G1 Y.75	N130 G1 Y.75
N140 G3 X.75 Y1. I-.25 J0. (0.5 Radius)	N140 G3 X.75 Y1. R.25 (0.5 Radius)
N150 G0 Z.35	N150 G0 Z.35

Review the program to machine the contour shown below.

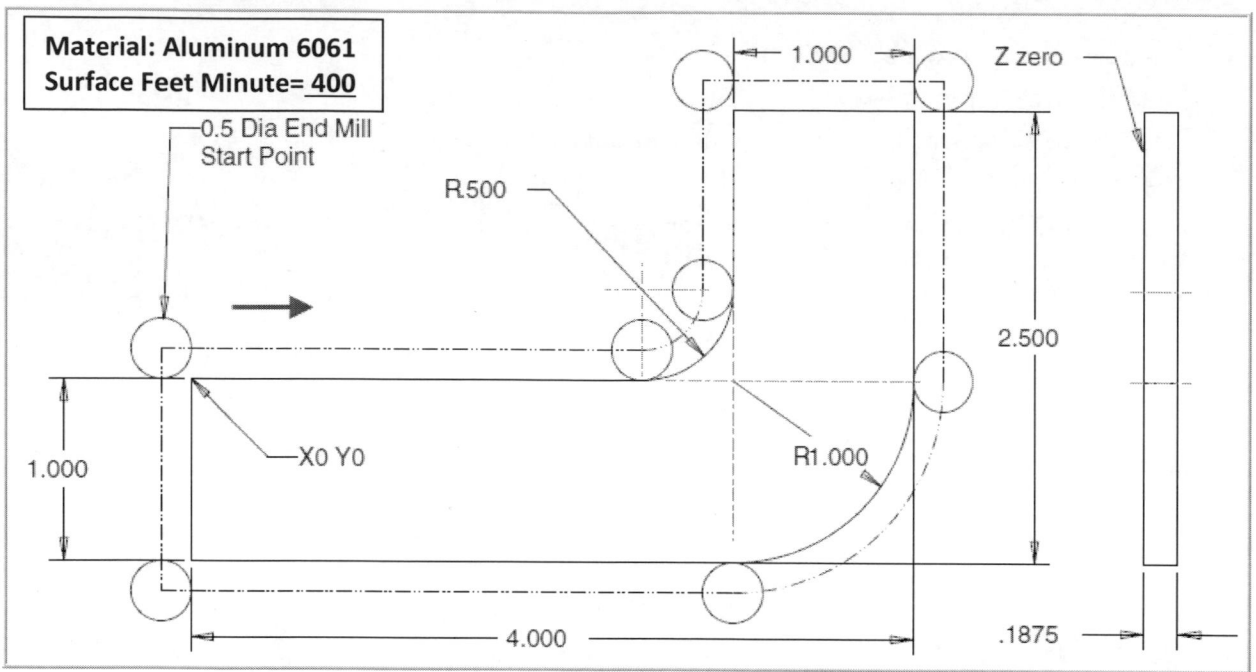

Tool #4 (Ø.500" Flat End Mill) – Mill the profile	
Spindle Speed RPM = 3.82xSFM/D= 3.82x400/0.5 =3056	Feed Per Tooth (FPT) = 0.003 – 2 Flute Cutter Feed Per Minute = FPT x 2 Flutes x RPM = 18.336
Depth of Cut = Z-0.200	Start from the top left corner

%	
O11　　　　　　　(G02-G03-EXAMPLE)	N60 X4.25
N10 G20	N65 Y0.
N15 G0 G17 G40 G49 G80 G90	N70 G2 X3. Y-1.25 I-1.25 J0.
N20 T4 M6	N75 G1 X-.25
N25 G0 G90 G54 X-.25 Y.25 S3056 M3	N80 Y.25
N30 G43 H4 Z2.	N85 G0 Z2.
N35 Z.1	N90 M5
N40 G1 Z-.2 F18.	N95 G91 G28 Z0.
N45 X2.5	N100 G28 X0. Y0.
N50 G3 X2.75 Y.5 I0. J.25	N105 M30
N55 G1 Y1.75	%

Create the program to machine the contour shown below.

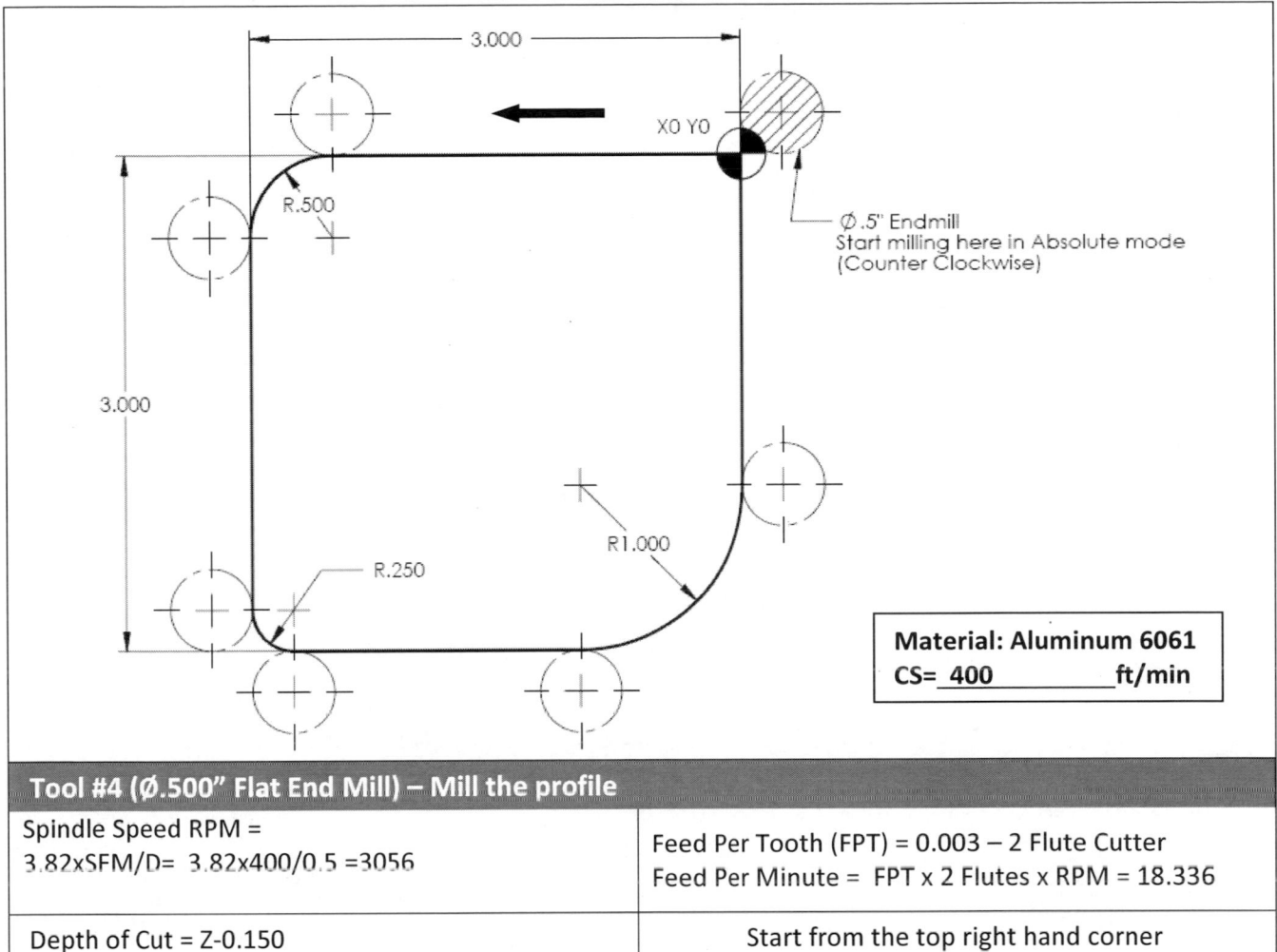

Ø.5" Endmill
Start milling here in Absolute mode
(Counter Clockwise)

Material: Aluminum 6061
CS= 400   ft/min

Tool #4 (Ø.500" Flat End Mill) – Mill the profile

Spindle Speed RPM = 3.82xSFM/D= 3.82x400/0.5 =3056	Feed Per Tooth (FPT) = 0.003 – 2 Flute Cutter Feed Per Minute = FPT x 2 Flutes x RPM = 18.336
Depth of Cut = Z-0.150	Start from the top right hand corner

%
O12

CNC PROGRAMMING

WORKBOOK

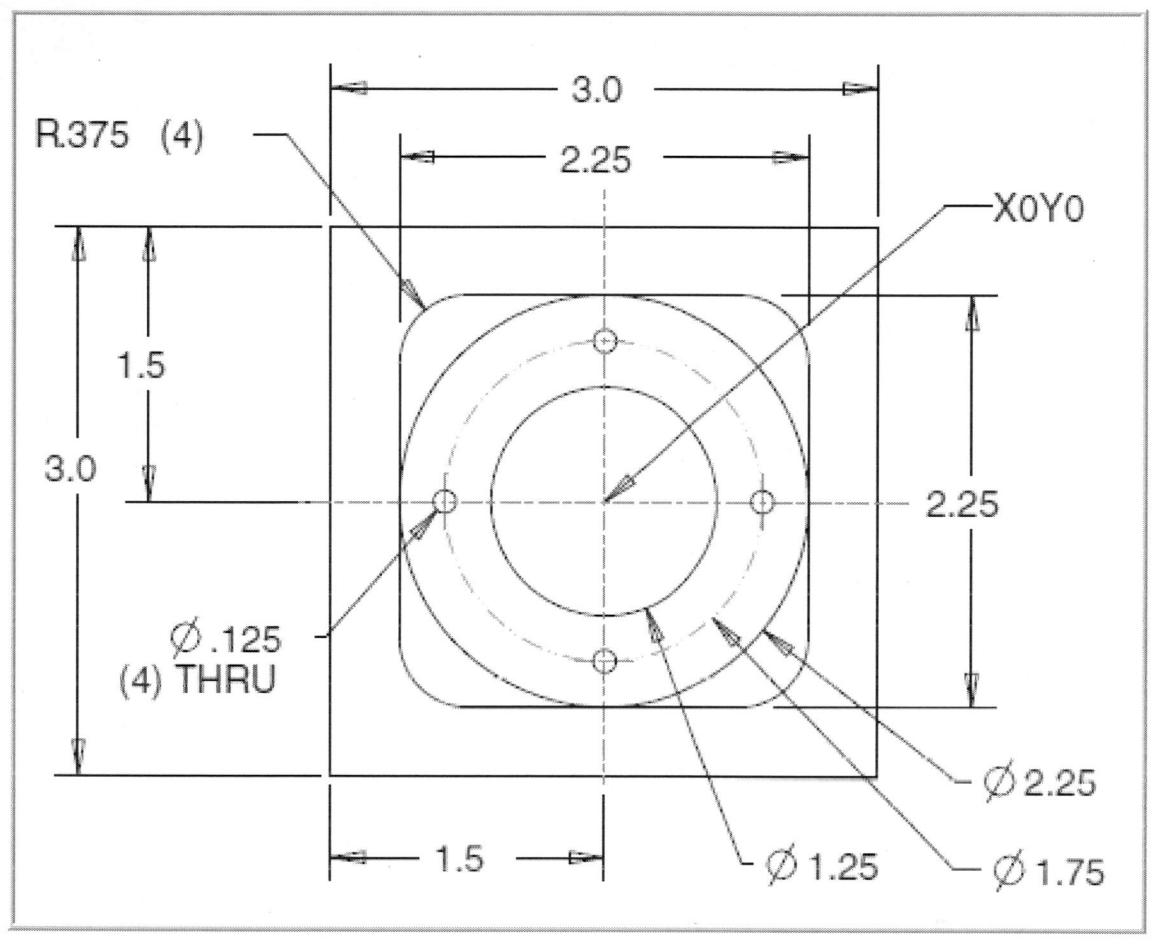

MILL-LESSON-8

CIRCULAR INTERPOLATION - CONTINUED

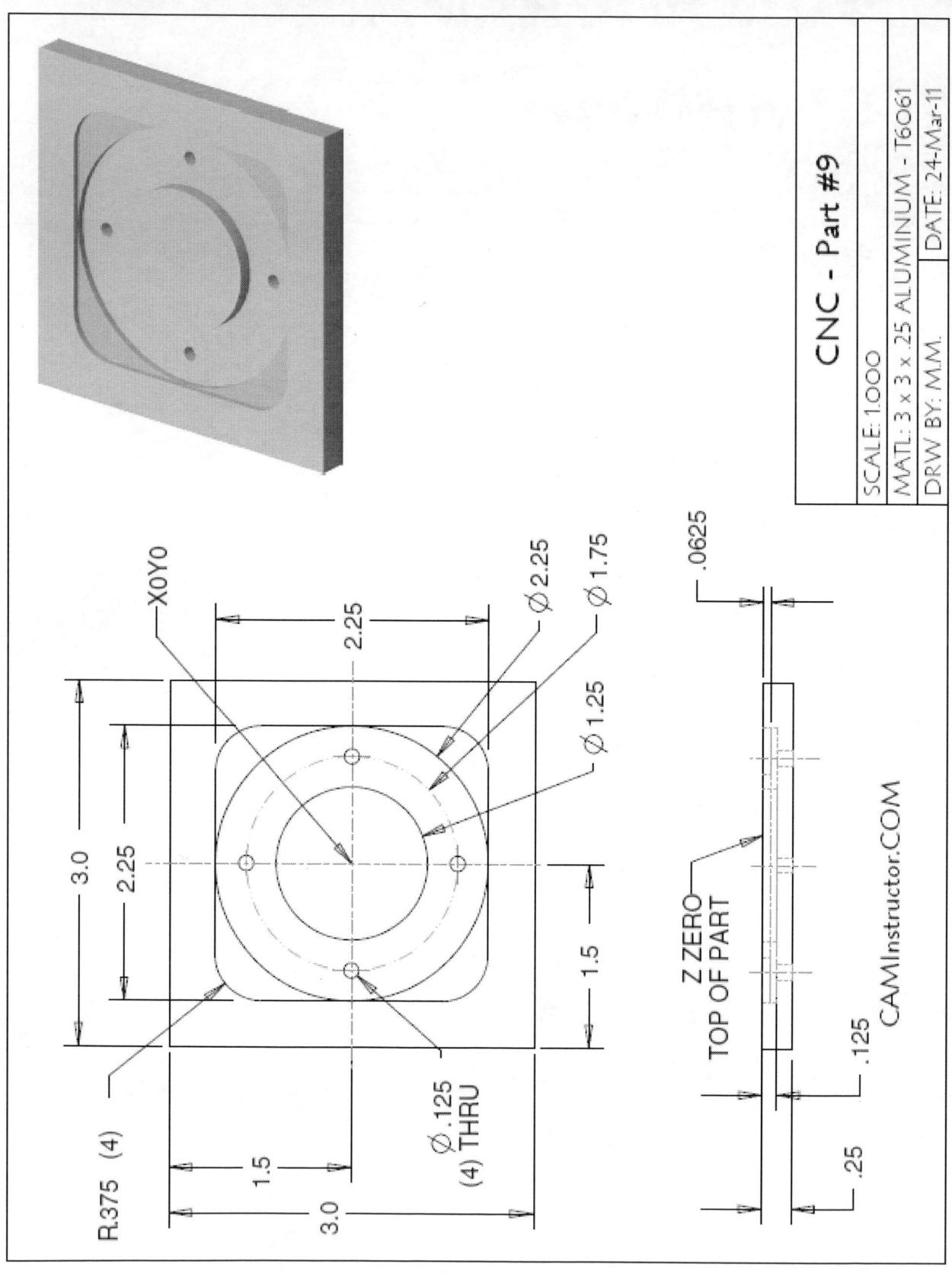

CNC - Part #9

SCALE: 1.000
MATL: 3 x 3 x .25 ALUMINUM - T6061
DRW BY: MM.   DATE: 24-Mar-11

CAMInstructor.COM

- ### *The Machining Process*
- **Ø.500" Endmill - Tool # 4 - 3056 RPM Feedrate 18 IPM**
  - Machine the 2.25" square with the 0.375" corner radii - 0.0625" depth
  - Machine the circular 2.25" and 1.25"diameter circular profile - 0.125" depth
- **Ø.125" Endmill - Tool # 1- 5000 RPM Feedrate 7 IPM**
  - Drill the Ø .125" holes through the part (4 places)
  - **Note:** The Ø.125" Endmill is designed for center cutting machining. No center drilling or pilot hole is required.

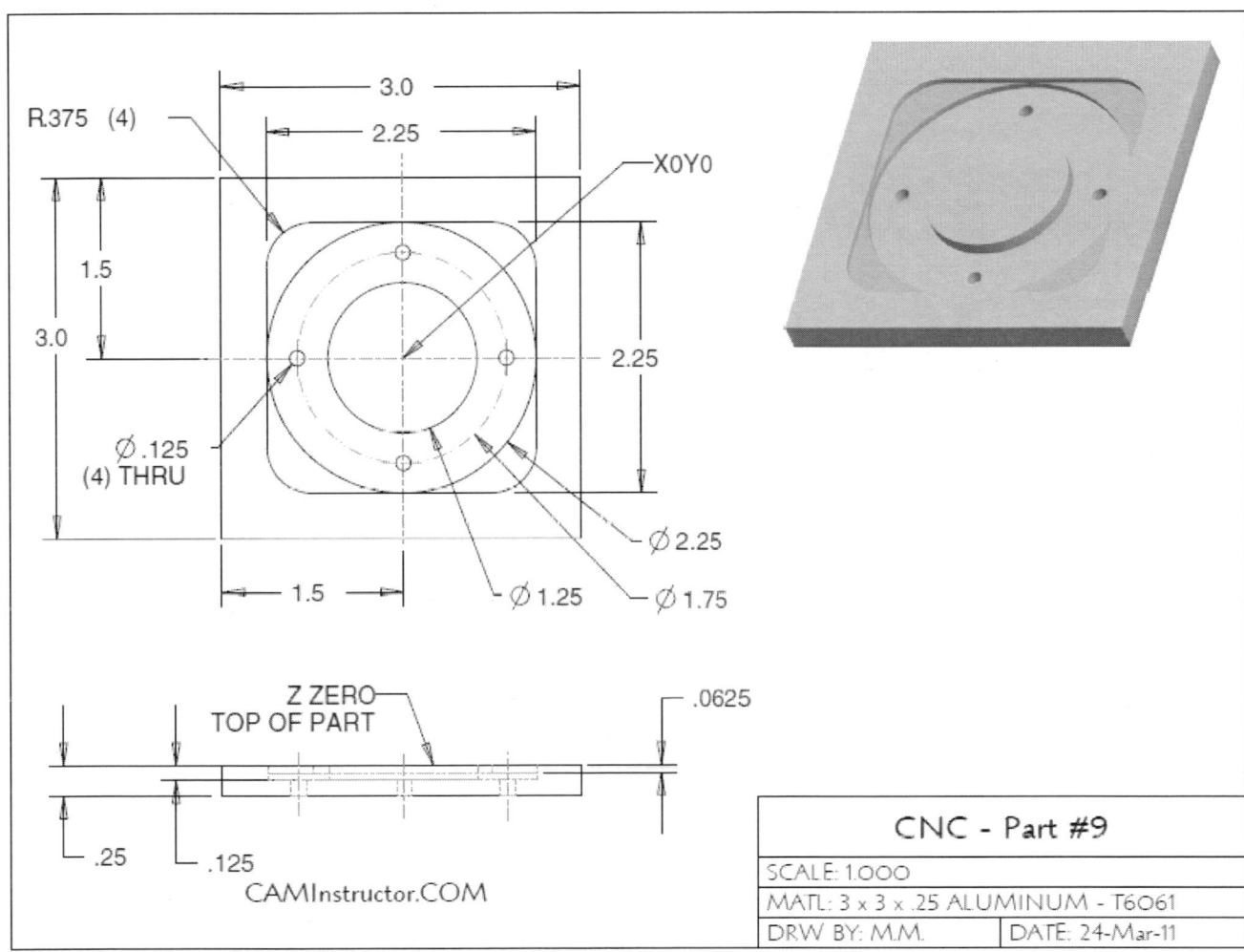

CAMInstructor.COM

CNC - Part #9	
SCALE: 1.000	
MATL: 3 x 3 x .25 ALUMINUM - T6061	
DRW BY: M.M.	DATE: 24-Mar-11

- **WORK OUT THE ABSOLUTE X AND Y COORDINATES FOR THE VARIOUS POSITIONS TO MACHINE THE PART**
  - X0Y0 is at the center of the part
  - Use a 0.5" diameter End Mill Tool # 4 and a 0.125" diameter End Mill Tool # 1
  - Climb mill the inside contours

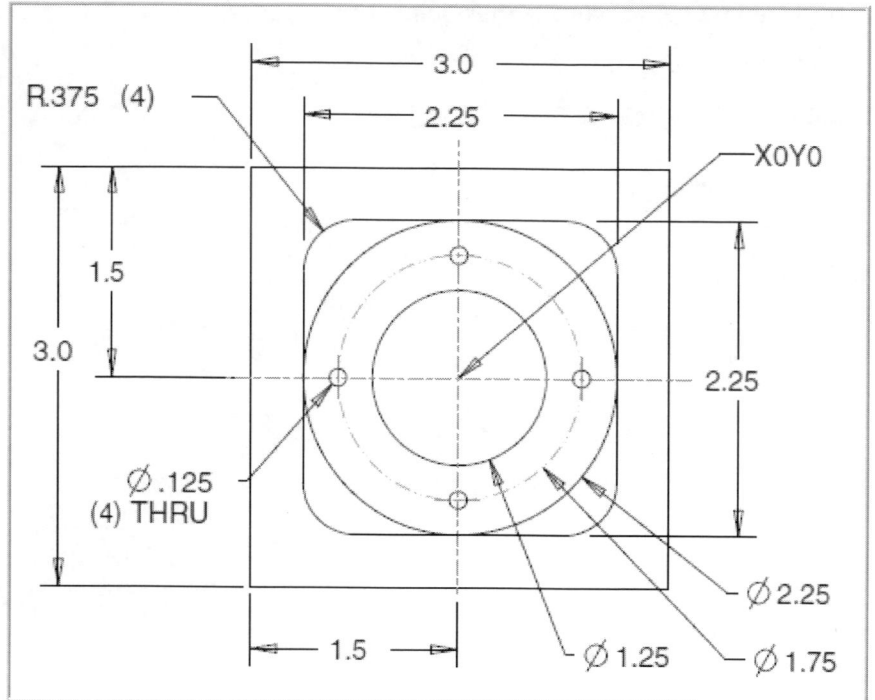
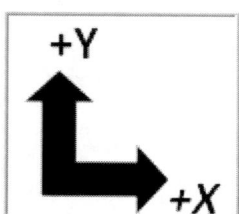

- **WORK OUT THE ABSOLUTE X AND Y COORDINATES FOR THE FOUR HOLES**

G90	X	Y
1		
2		
3		
4		

- ***WORK OUT THE ABSOLUTE X AND Y COORDINATES FOR THE VARIOUS POSITIONS TO MACHINE THE PART***
  - X0Y0 is at the center of the part
  - Use a 0.5" diameter End Mill Tool # 4 and a 0.125" diameter End Mill Tool # 1
  - Climb mill

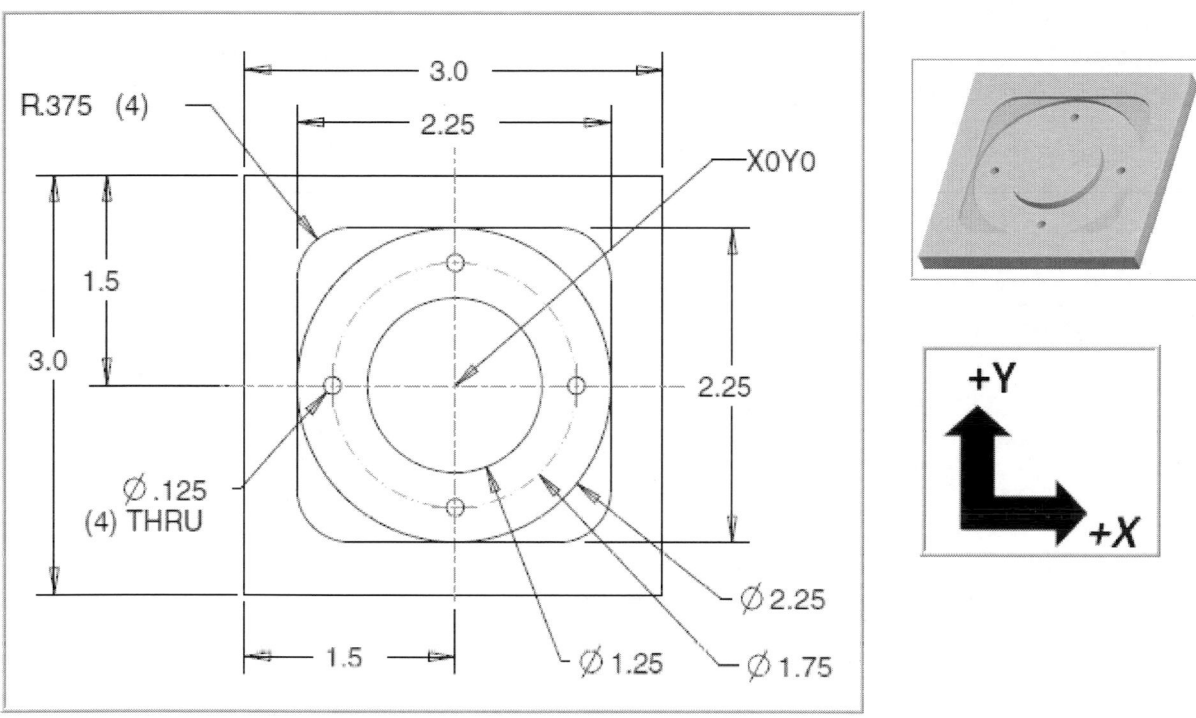

- ***WORK OUT THE ABSOLUTE X AND Y COORDINATES FOR THE VARIOUS POSITIONS OF THE 0.5" DIAMETER END MILL***

G90	X	Y
1		
2		
3		
4		
5		
6		
7		
8		
9		
10		
11		

- **CREATE THE PROGRAM TO MACHINE THE PART**
    - Use a 0.5" diameter End Mill Tool # 4
    - Speed = 3050 Feed rate =20 IPM
    - Use a 0.125" diameter End Mill Tool # 1
    - Speed = 5000 Feed rate =7 IPM
    - X0Y0 is at the center of the part
    - Z=0 is the top of the part.
    - Climb mill
    - Type up your program and check it for correctness using the Simulation software.

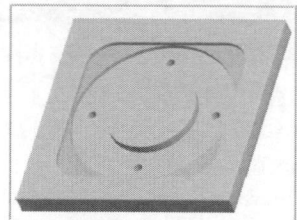

%	
O13	(CNC PART #9)
N10	G20
N20	G00 G17 G40 G49 G80 G90 (MACHINE DEFAULT SETTING)
N30	

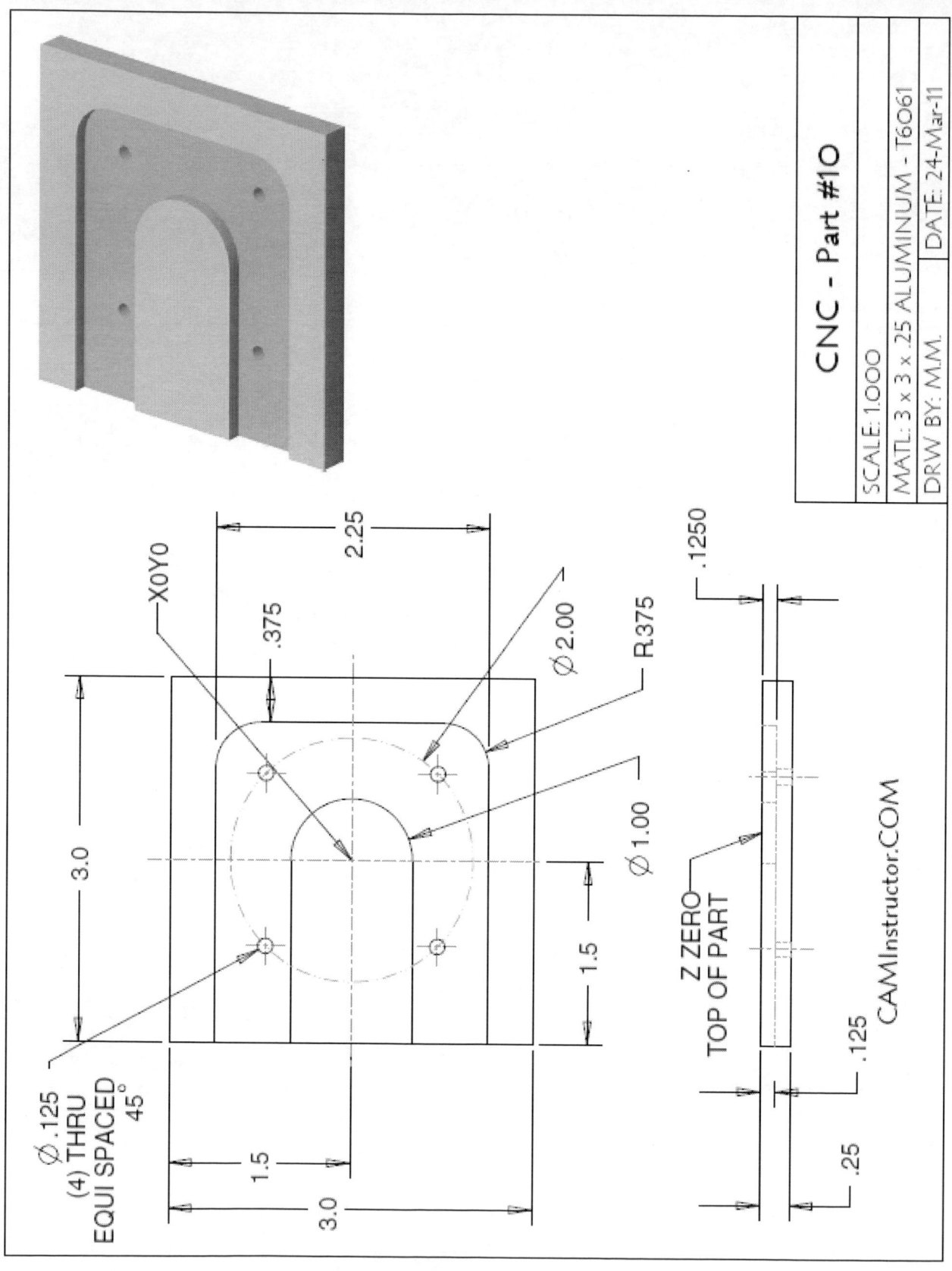

CNC - Part #10

SCALE: 1.000
MATL: 3 x 3 x .25 ALUMINUM - T6061
DRW BY: MM.   DATE: 24-Mar-11

X0Y0

.375

2.25

Ø 2.00

R375

Ø 1.00

3.0

1.5

Ø .125
(4) THRU
EQUI SPACED
45°

1.5

3.0

.1250

Z ZERO
TOP OF PART

.125

.25

CAMInstructor.COM

- ### *The Machining Process*
- ### *Ø.500" Endmill - Tool # 4 - 3056 RPM Feedrate 18 IPM*
  - Machine the open slot with the 0.375" fillet radii - 0.125" depth
- ### *Ø.125" Endmill - Tool # 1 - 5000 RPM Feedrate 7 IPM*
  - Drill the Ø .125" holes through the part (4 places)
  - **Note:** The Ø.125" Endmill is designed for center cutting machining. No center drilling or pilot hole is required.

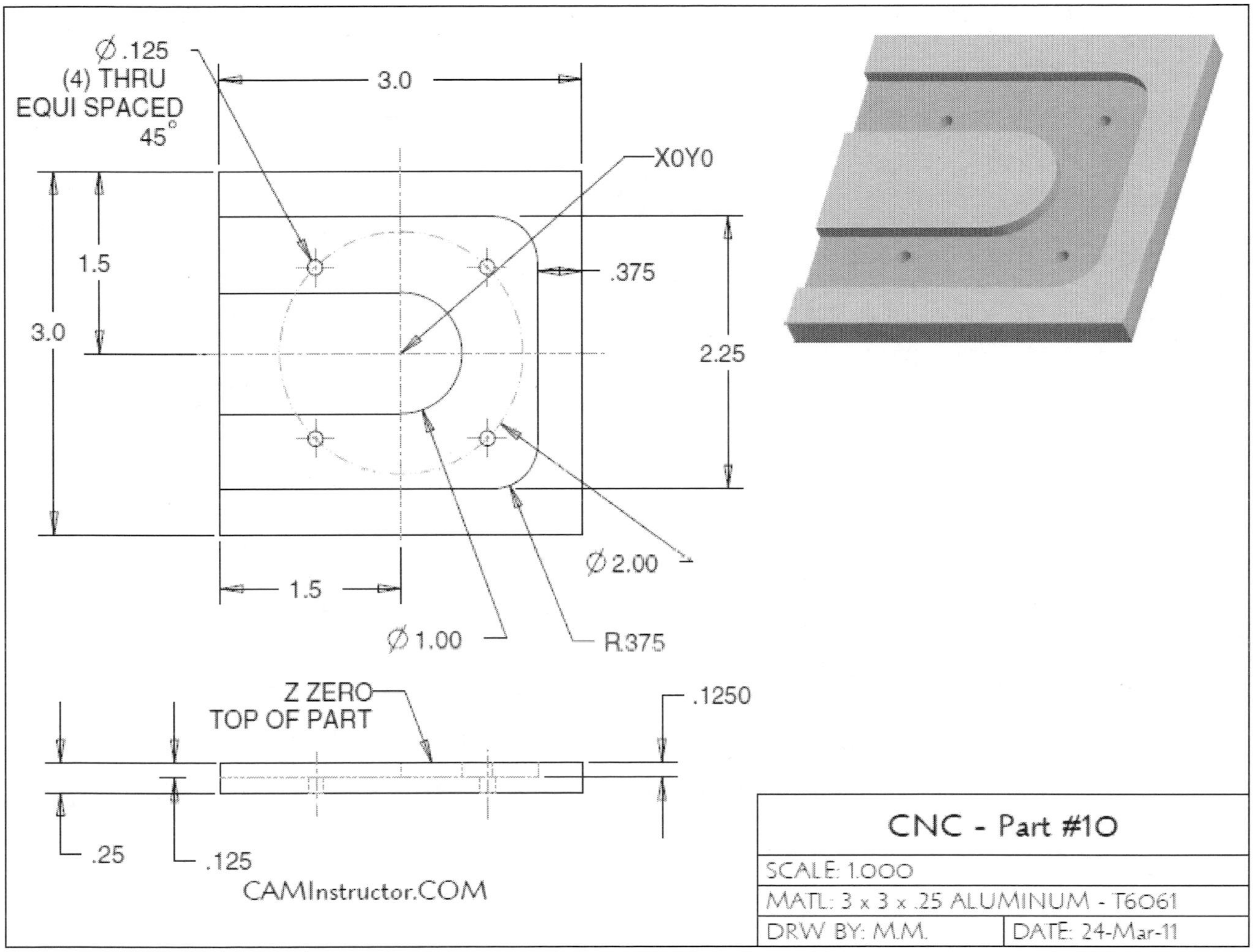

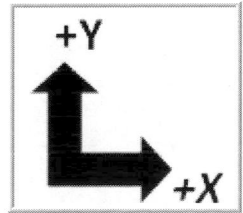

- **WORK OUT THE ABSOLUTE X AND Y COORDINATES FOR THE VARIOUS POSITIONS TO MACHINE THE PART**
  - X0Y0 is at the center of the part
  - Use a 0.5" diameter End Mill Tool # 4 and a 0.125" diameter End Mill Tool # 1

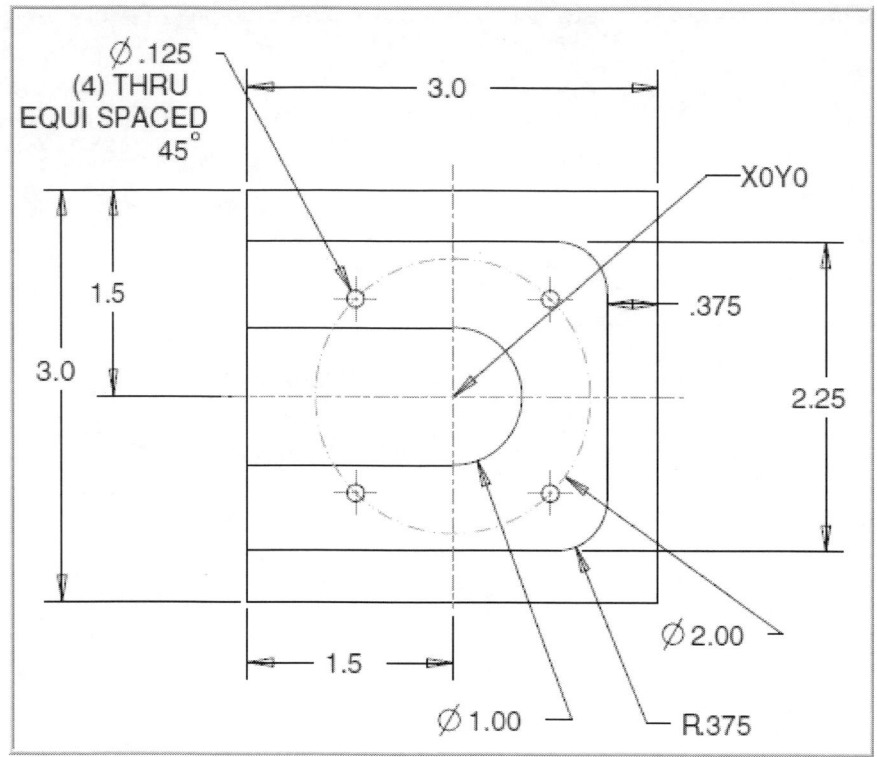

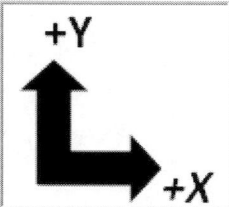

- **WORK OUT THE ABSOLUTE X AND Y COORDINATES FOR THE FOUR HOLES**

G90	X	Y
1		
2		
3		
4		

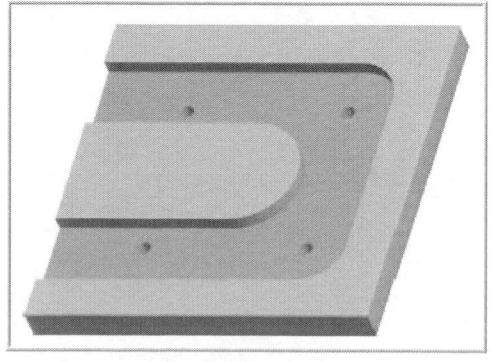

- **WORK OUT THE ABSOLUTE X AND Y COORDINATES FOR THE VARIOUS POSITIONS TO MACHINE THE PART**
  - X0Y0 is at the center of the part
  - Use a 0.5" diameter End Mill Tool # 4 and a 0.125" diameter End Mill Tool # 1
  - Climb mill

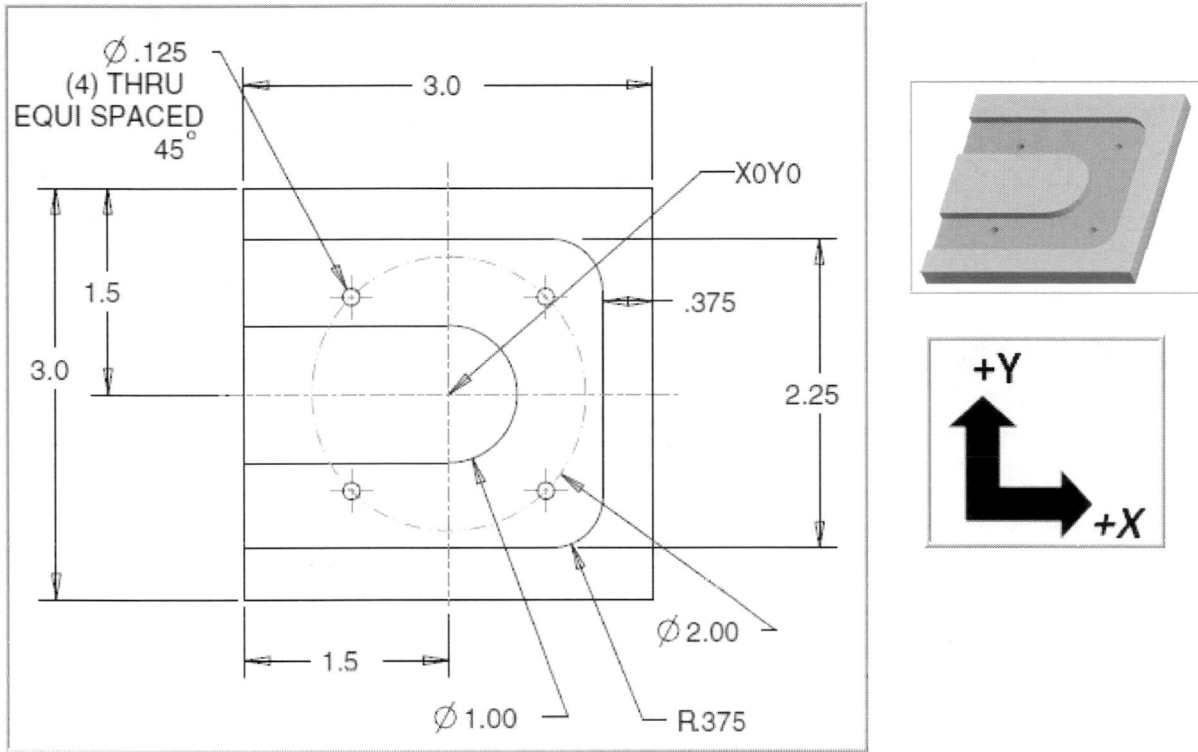

- **WORK OUT THE ABSOLUTE X AND Y COORDINATES FOR THE VARIOUS POSITIONS OF THE 0.5' DIAMETER END MILL**

G90	X	Y
1		
2		
3		
4		
5		
6		
7		
8		
9		
10		

- **CREATE THE PROGRAM TO MACHINE THE PART**
  - Use a 0.5" diameter End Mill Tool # 4
  - Speed = 3050 Feed rate =20 IPM
  - Use a 0.125" diameter End Mill Tool # 1
  - Speed = 5000 Feed rate =7 IPM
  - X0Y0 is at the center of the part
  - Z=0 is the top of the part.
  - Climb mill
  - Type up your program and check it for correctness using the Simulation software.

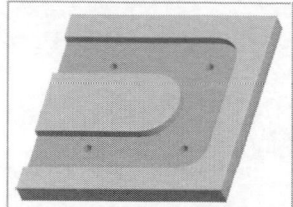

%	
O003	
N10	G20
N20	G00 G17 G40 G49 G80 G90 (MACHINE DEFAULT SETTING)
N30	

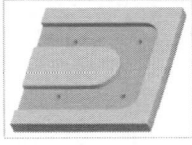

CNC PROGRAMMING

WORKBOOK

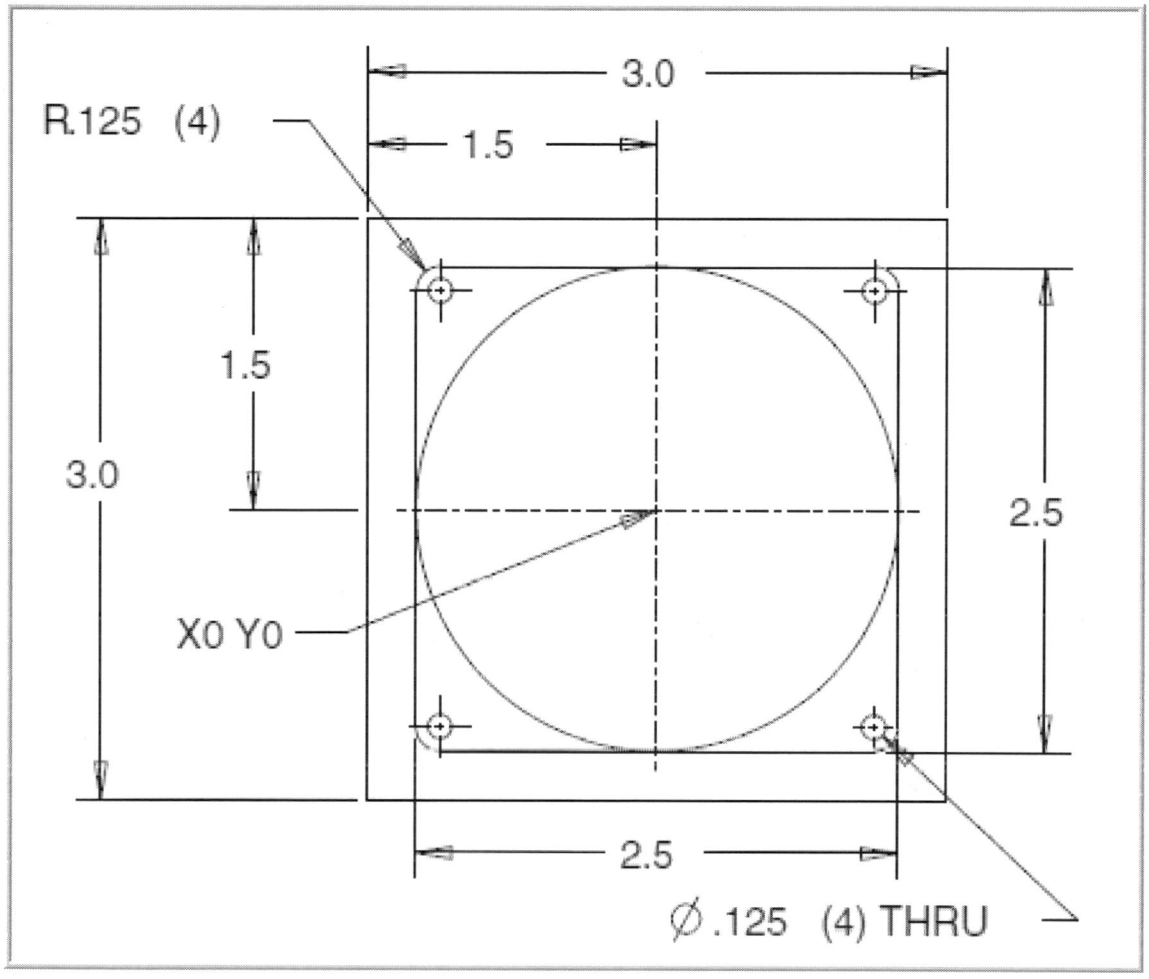

LESSON-9

CIRCULAR INTERPOLATION - CONTINUED

camInstructor

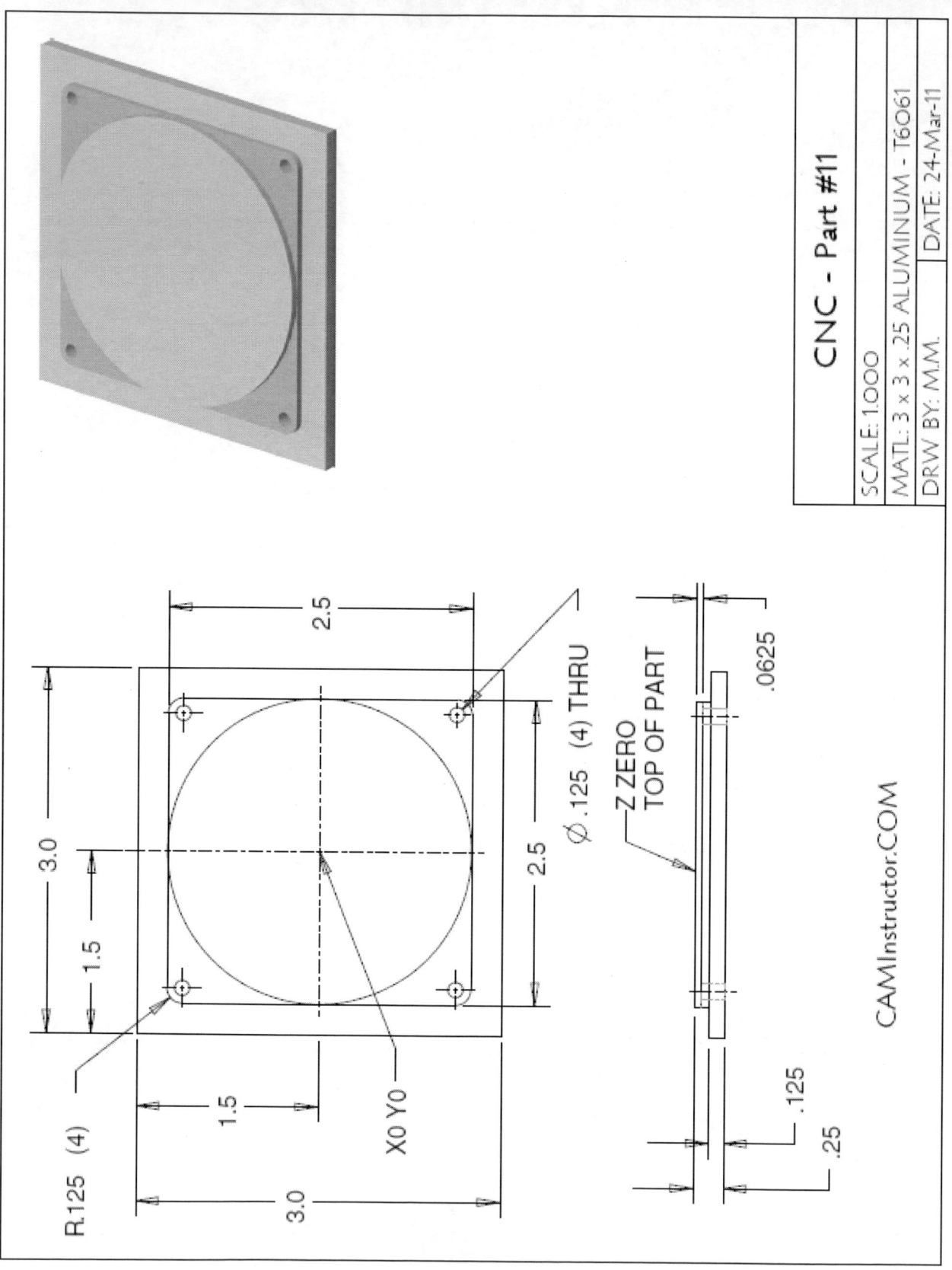

CNC - Part #11

SCALE: 1.000
MATL: 3 x 3 x .25 ALUMINUM - T6061
DRW BY: M.M.   DATE: 24-Mar-11

CAMInstructor.COM

- **The Machining Process**
- **Ø.500" Endmill - Tool # 4**
  - Machine the profile with the .125" radii at Z-.125" deep – 1 Cut
  - Machine the circular 2.5" diameter circular profile – 1 Cut
- **Ø.125" Endmill - Tool # 1**
  - Drill the Ø .125" holes through the part (4 places)
  - **Note:** The Ø.125" Endmill is designed for center cutting machining. No center drilling or pilot hole is required.

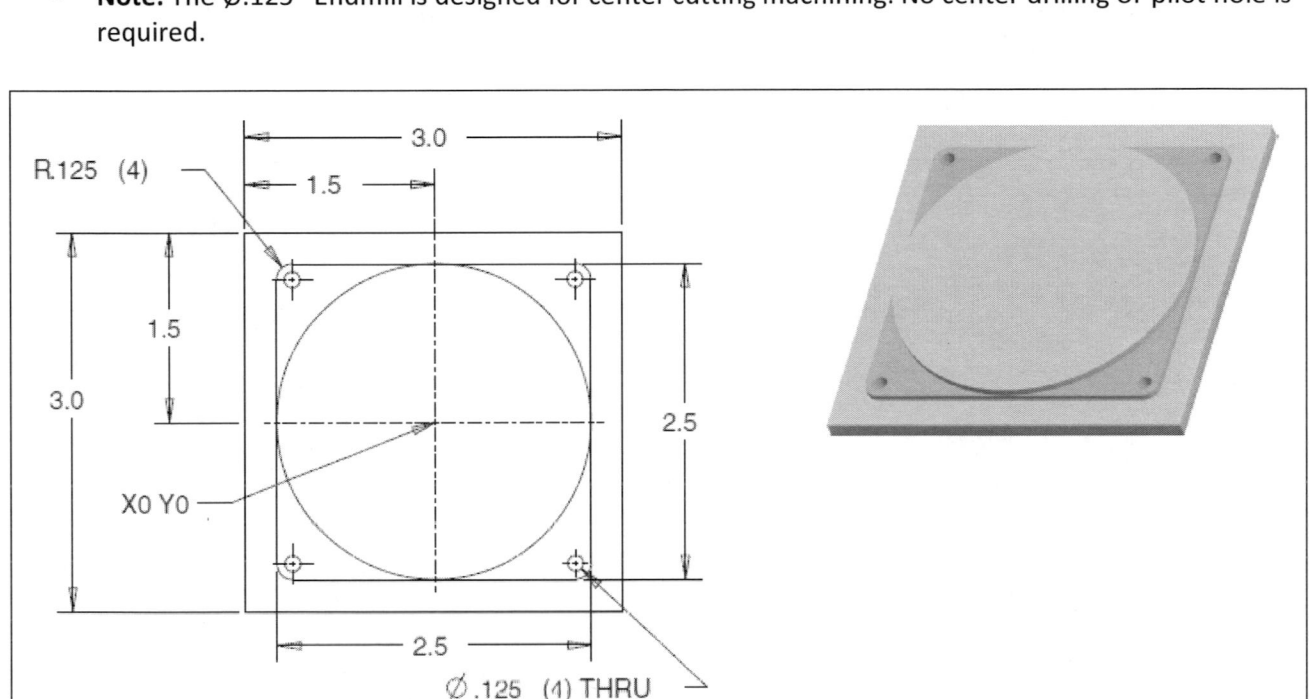

R.125 (4)

3.0
1.5

1.5

3.0

X0 Y0

2.5

2.5

Ø .125 (4) THRU

Z ZERO
TOP OF PART

.0625

.125

.25

CAMInstructor.COM

CNC - Part #11	
SCALE: 1.000	
MATL: 3 x 3 x .25 ALUMINUM - T6061	
DRW BY: M.M.	DATE: 24-Mar-11

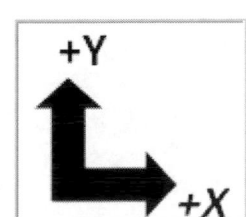

+Y
+X

- **WORK OUT THE ABSOLUTE X AND Y COORDINATES FOR THE VARIOUS POSITIONS TO MACHINE THE PART**
  - X0Y0 is at the center of the part
  - Use a 0.5" diameter End Mill Tool # 4 and a 0.125" diameter End Mill Tool # 1

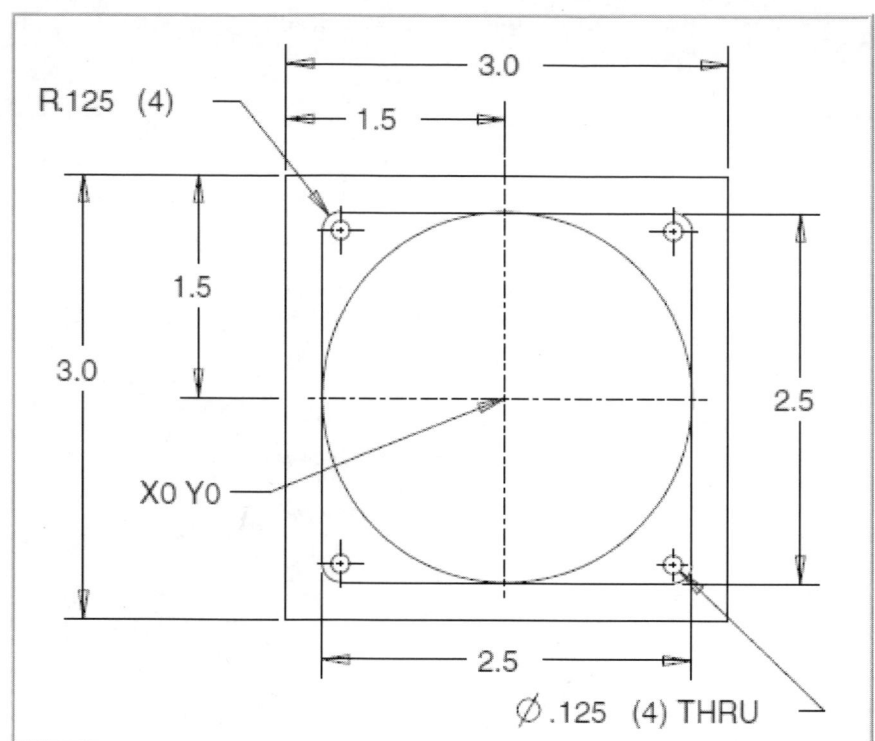

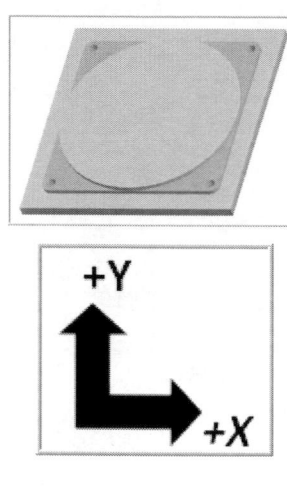

- **WORK OUT THE ABSOLUTE X AND Y COORDINATES FOR THE FOUR HOLES**

G90	X	Y
1		
2		
3		
4		

- ***WORK OUT THE ABSOLUTE X AND Y COORDINATES FOR THE VARIOUS POSITIONS TO MACHINE THE PART***
  - XOYO is at the center of the part
  - Use a 0.5" diameter End Mill Tool # 4 and a 0.125" diameter End Mill Tool # 1
  - Climb mill

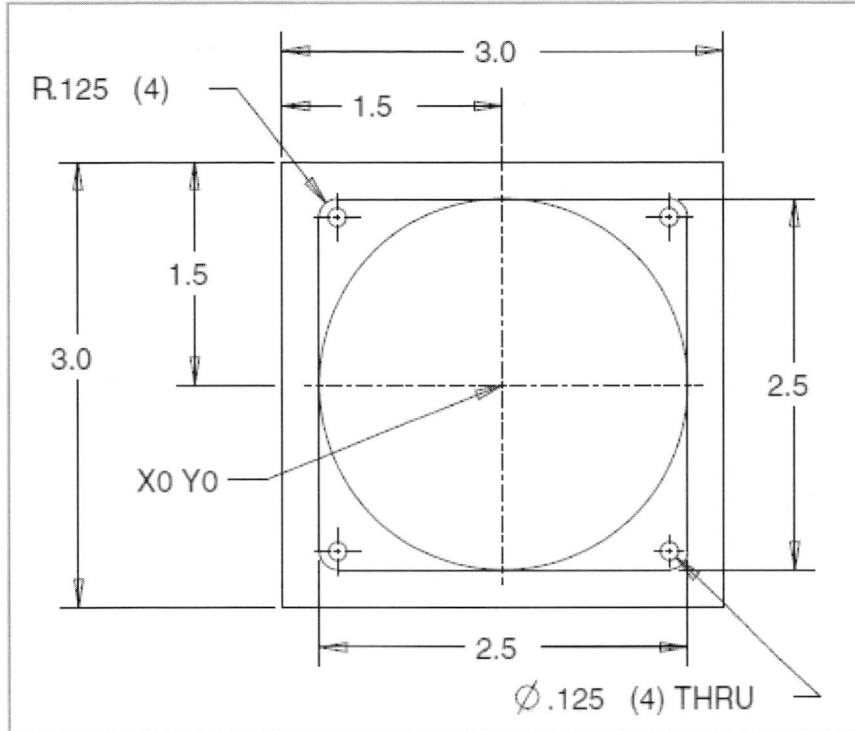

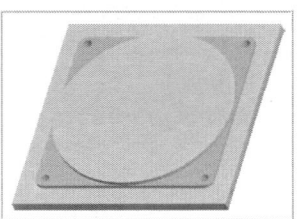

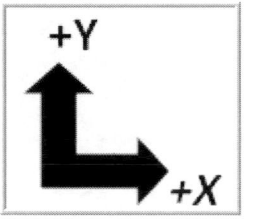

- ***WORK OUT THE ABSOLUTE X AND Y COORDINATES FOR THE VARIOUS POSITIONS OF THE 0.5' DIAMETER END MILL***

G90	X	Y
1		
2		
3		
4		
5		
6		
7		
8		
9		
10		

LESSON-9 - CNC - PART #11

- ***CREATE THE PROGRAM TO MACHINE THE PART***
  - Use a 0.5" diameter End Mill Tool # 4
  - Speed = 3050 Feed rate =20 IPM
  - Use a 0.125" diameter End Mill Tool # 1
  - Speed = 5000 Feed rate =7 IPM
  - X0Y0 is at the center of the part
  - Z=0 is the top of the part.
  - Climb mill
  - Type up your program and check it for correctness using the Simulation software.

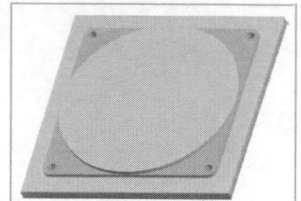

%
O003
N10 G20
N20 G00 G17 G40 G49 G80 G90 (MACHINE DEFAULT SETTING)
N30

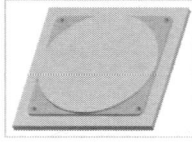

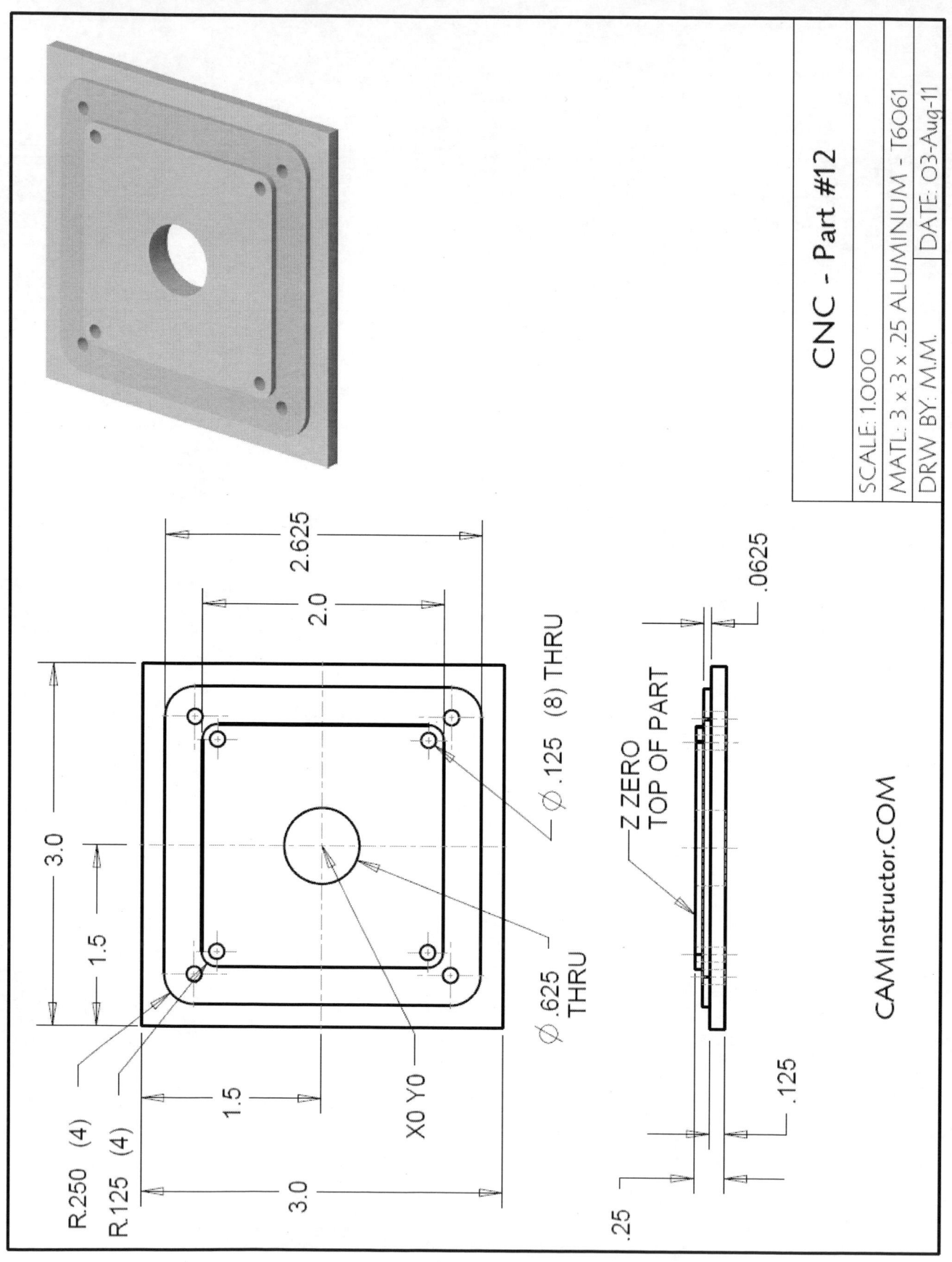

CNC - Part #12

SCALE: 1.000
MATL: 3 x 3 x .25 ALUMINUM - T6061
DRW BY: M.M.   DATE: 03-Aug-11

2.625
2.0
3.0
1.5
R.250 (4)
R.125 (4)
1.5
X0 Y0
3.0

Ø.125 (8) THRU
Ø.625 THRU

Z ZERO
TOP OF PART
.0625
.125
.25

CAMInstructor.COM

- ***The Machining Process***
- ***Ø.500" Endmill - Tool # 4- 3050 RPM Feedrate 20 IPM***
  - Machine the profiles with the .125" and .25 radii.
  - Machine the circular 0.625" diameter through hole. Sink to depth at center and use circular interpolation to finish the bore.
- ***Ø.125" Endmill - Tool # 1- 5000 RPM Feedrate 7 IPM***
  - Drill the Ø .125" holes through the part (8 places)
  - **Note:** The Ø.125" Endmill is designed for center cutting machining. No center drilling or pilot hole is required.

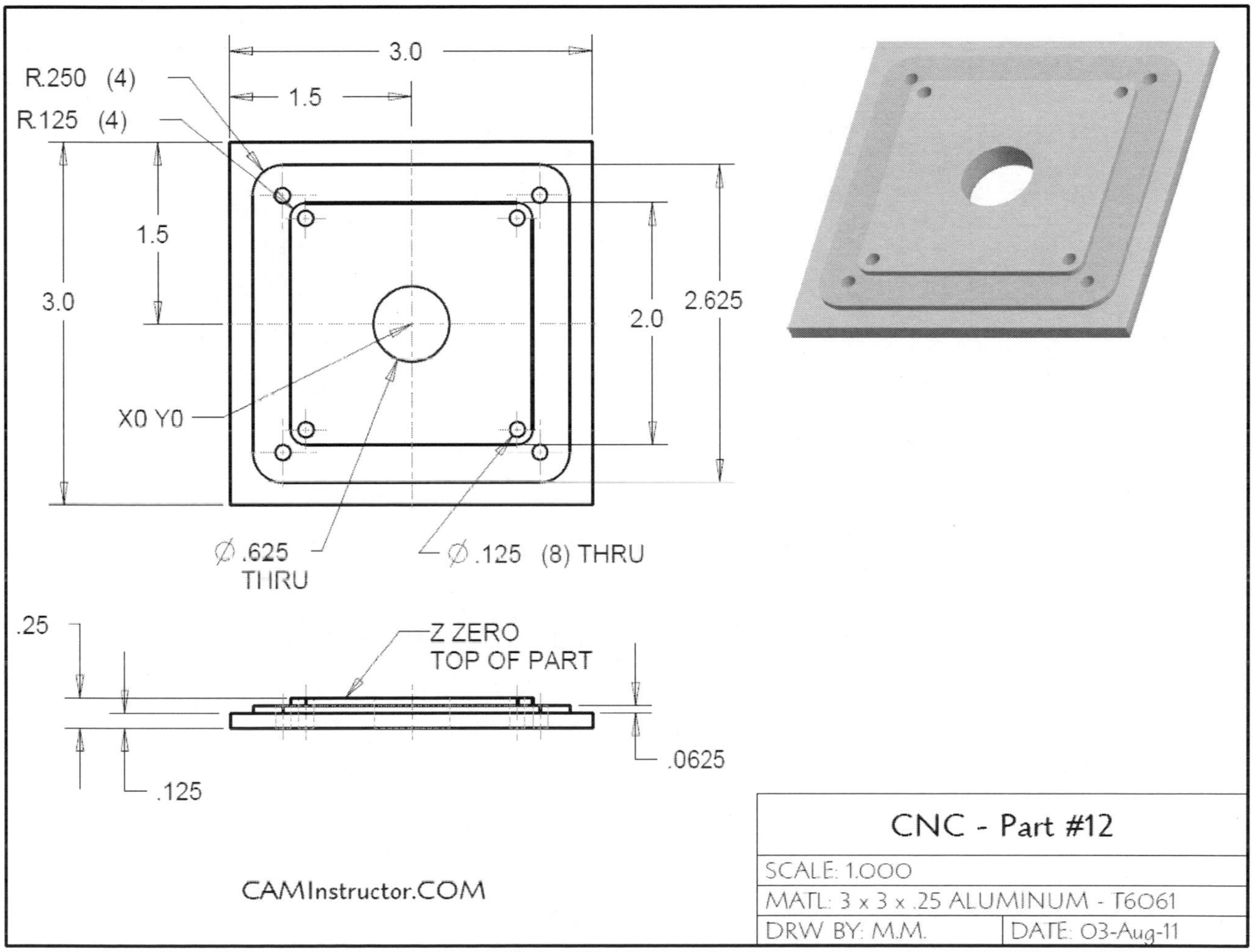

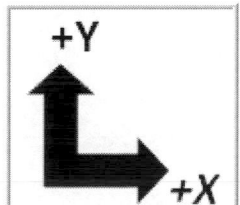

3.0
1.5
R.250 (4)
R.125 (4)
1.5
3.0
2.0
2.625
X0 Y0
Ø.625
THRU
Ø.125 (8) THRU
.25
Z ZERO
TOP OF PART
.0625
.125
CAMInstructor.COM
CNC - Part #12
SCALE: 1.000
MATL: 3 x 3 x .25 ALUMINUM - T6061
DRW BY: M.M.
DATE: 03-Aug-11

+Y
+X

- **WORK OUT THE ABSOLUTE X AND Y COORDINATES FOR THE VARIOUS POSITIONS TO MACHINE THE PART**
  - X0Y0 is at the center of the part
  - Use a 0.5" diameter End Mill Tool # 4 and a 0.125" diameter End Mill Tool # 1

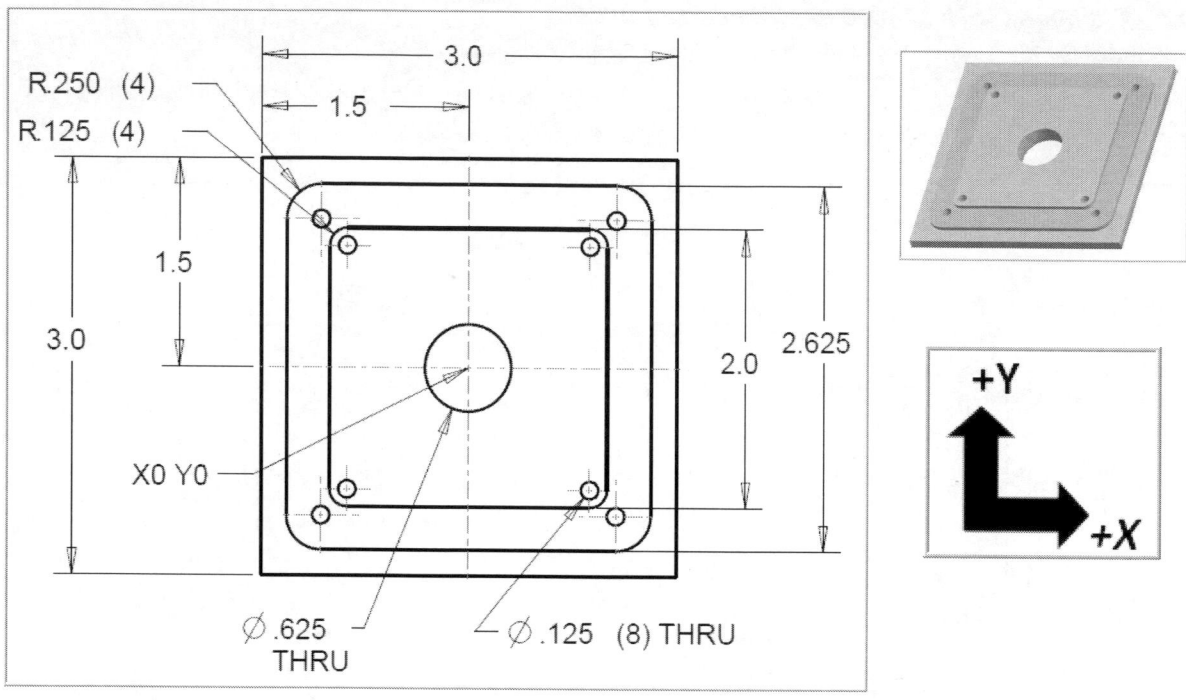

- **WORK OUT THE ABSOLUTE X AND Y COORDINATES FOR THE HOLES**

G90	X	Y
1	0	0
2		
3		
4		
5		
6		
7		
8		
9		

- ### WORK OUT THE ABSOLUTE X AND Y COORDINATES FOR THE VARIOUS POSITIONS TO MACHINE THE PART
    - XOYO is at the center of the part
    - Use a 0.5" diameter End Mill Tool # 4 and a 0.125" diameter End Mill Tool # 1
    - Climb mill

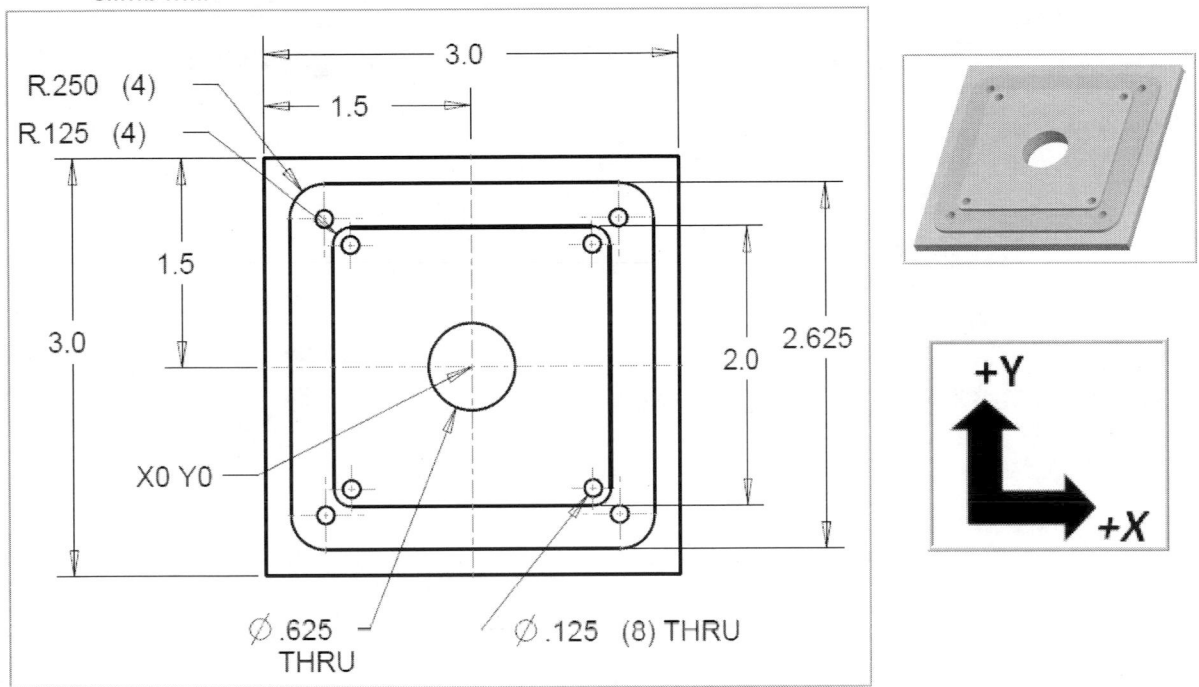

- ### WORK OUT THE ABSOLUTE X AND Y COORDINATES FOR THE VARIOUS POSITIONS OF THE 0.5' DIAMETER END MILL

2.625" Square Coordinates			2.0" Square Coordinates		
G90	X	Y	G90	X	Y
1			1		
2			2		
3			3		
4			4		
5			5		
6			6		
7			7		
8			8		
9			9		

- **CREATE THE PROGRAM TO MACHINE THE PART**
    - Use a 0.5" diameter End Mill Tool # 4
    - Speed = 3050 Feed rate =20 IPM
    - Use a 0.125" diameter End Mill Tool # 1
    - Speed = 5000 Feed rate =7 IPM
    - X0Y0 is at the center of the part
    - Z=0 is the top of the part.
    - Climb mill
    - Type up your program and check it for correctness using the Simulation software.

%
O003
N10   G20
N20   G00 G17 G40 G49 G80 G90 (MACHINE DEFAULT SETTING)
N30

CNC PROGRAMMING
WORKBOOK

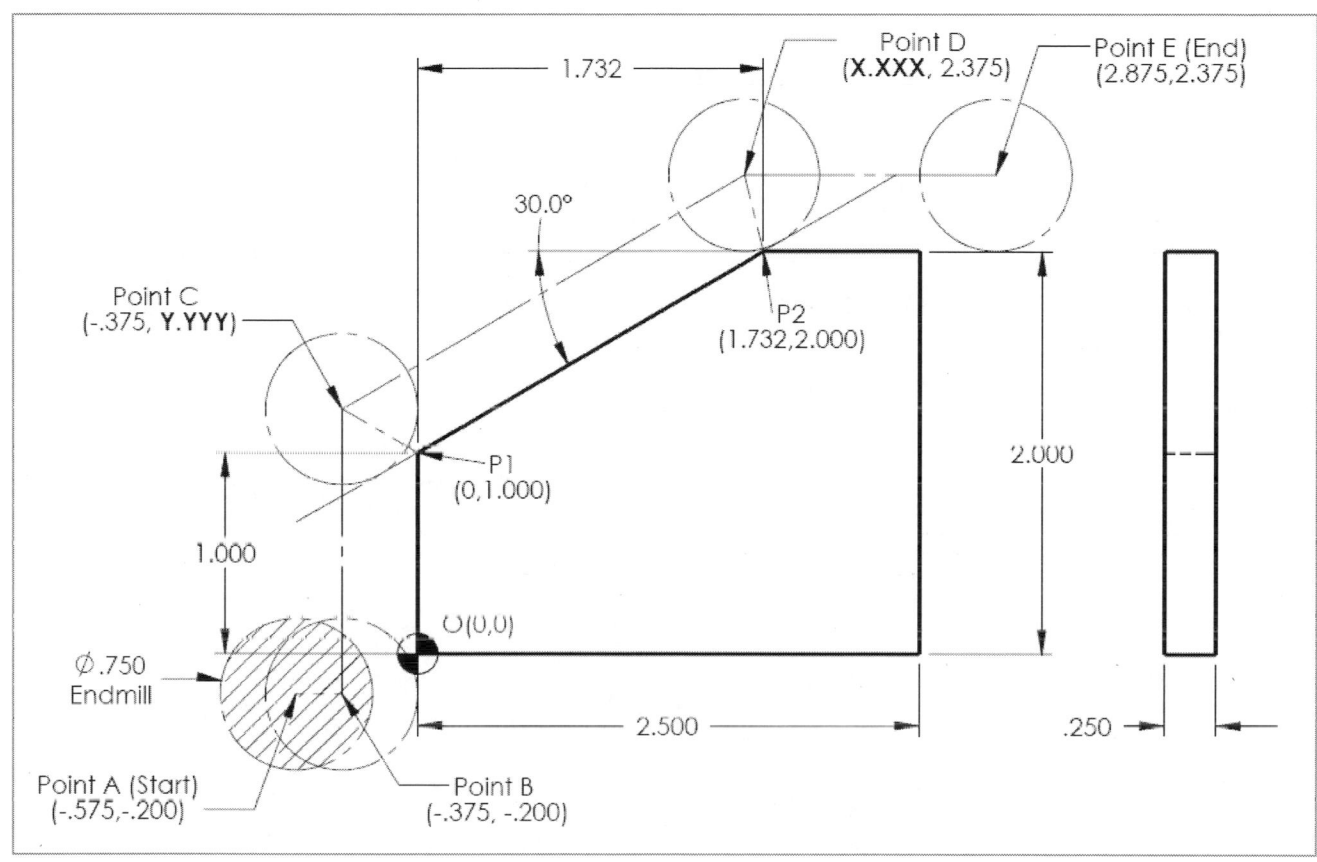

MILL-LESSON-10
CUTTER COMPENSATION

camInstructor

Cutter Compensation is used to offset the center of the cutter and move the cutter either to the left or right the distance of the cutter radius. When cutting angled geometry, substantial computations are required to determine the center of the cutter. Using Cutter Compensation, you can program the part as if the center of the cutter will be travelling along the geometry.

G40 CUTTER COMPENSATION CANCEL

G40 will cancel the G41 or G42 cutter compensation commands.

G41 CUTTER COMPENSATION LEFT

G41 will action cutter compensation left. The tool is moved to the left of the programmed path to compensate for the radius of the tool. A **Dnn** must also be programmed to select the correct tool size from the DIAMETER/RADIUS offset display register.

G42 CUTTER COMPENSATION RIGHT

G42 will action cutter compensation right. The tool is moved to the right of the programmed path to compensate for the size of the tool.

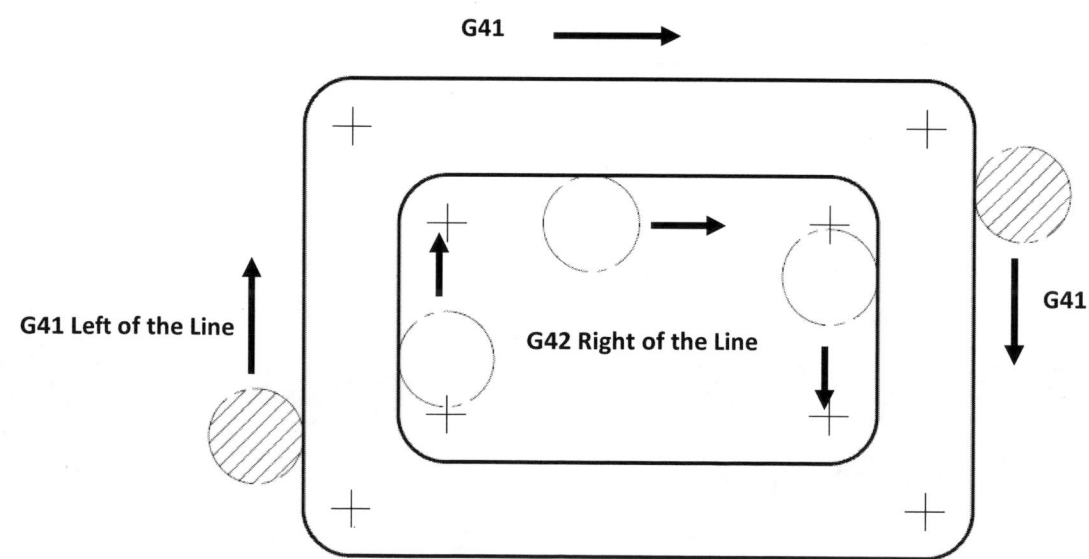

G41 : Tool is moved to the left of the profile (e.g. Outside Profile shown as above)
G42 : Tool is moved to the right of the profile (e.g. Inside Profile shown as above)

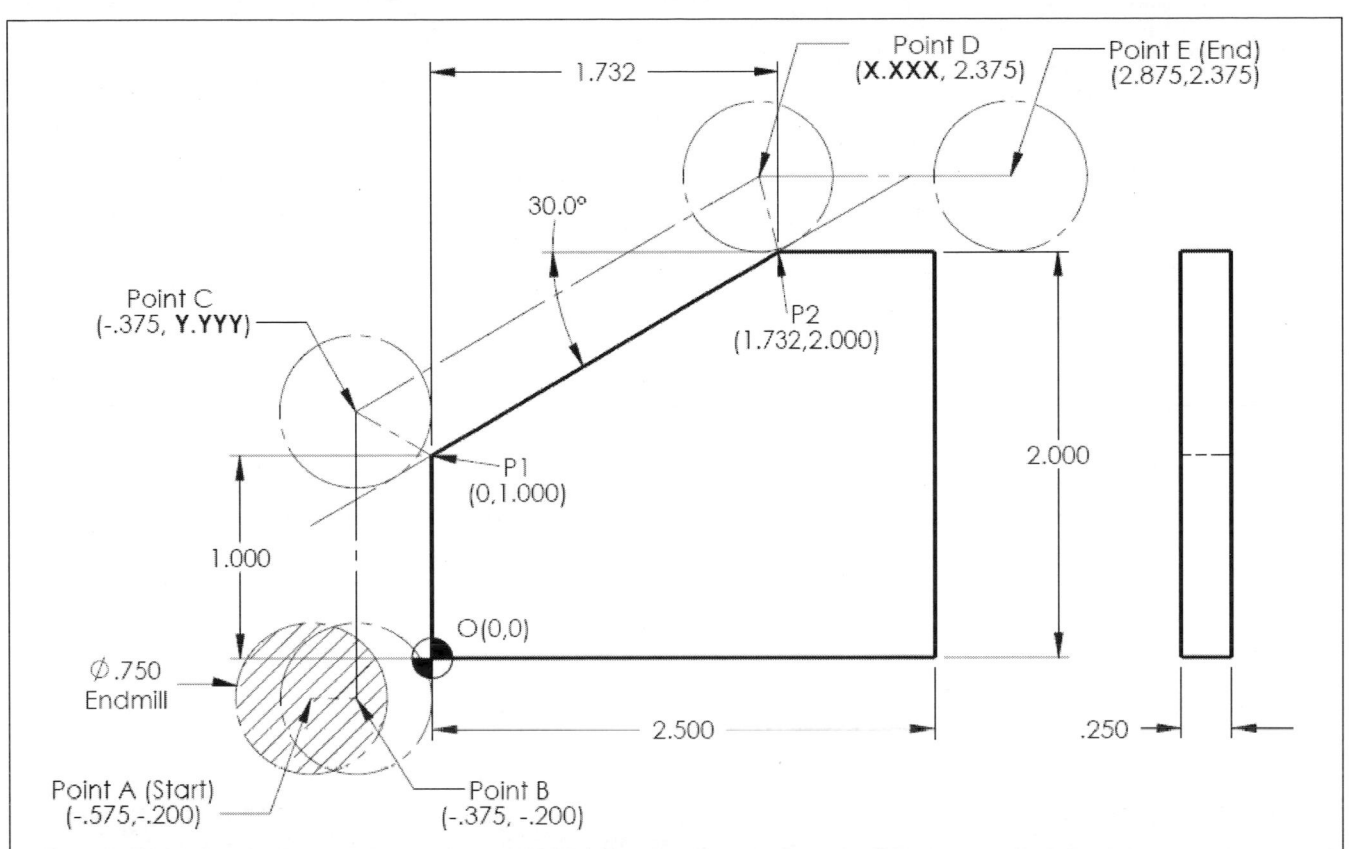

Without Cutter Compensation	Using Cutter Compensation
%	%
O10011	O10012
N1 T12 M06 (3/4" Flat Endmill)	N1 T12 M06 (3/4" Flat Endmill)
N2 G90 G54 G00 X-.575 Y-.200 S1500 M03	N2 G90 G54 G00 X-.575 Y-.200 S1500 M03
N3 G43 H12 Z2.	N3 G43 H12 Z2.
N4 Z.1	N4 Z.1
N5 G01 Z-.25 F10.	N5 G01 Z-.25 F10.
N6 X-.375 (Point B)	**N6 G41 X0. D12** (Origin)
N7 Y?.???? (Point C)	N7 Y1.0 (P1)
N8 X?.???? Y2.375 (Point D)	N8 X1.732 Y2.0 (P2)
N9 X2.875 (Point E)	N9 X2.875
N10 M05	**N10 G40 M05**
N11 G00 Z2.	N11 G00 Z2.
N12 G91 G28 Z0. (Machine Home Z-Axis)	N12 G91 G28 Z0. (Machine Home Z-Axis)
N13 G28 X0. Y0. (Machine Home X,Y-Axis)	N13 G28 X0. Y0. (Machine Home X,Y-Axis)
N14 M30	N14 M30
%	%

The Cutter Compensation (G41) will reflect the actual part geometry (O, P1, P2..) instead of Cutter Centers (Point B,C,D & E)

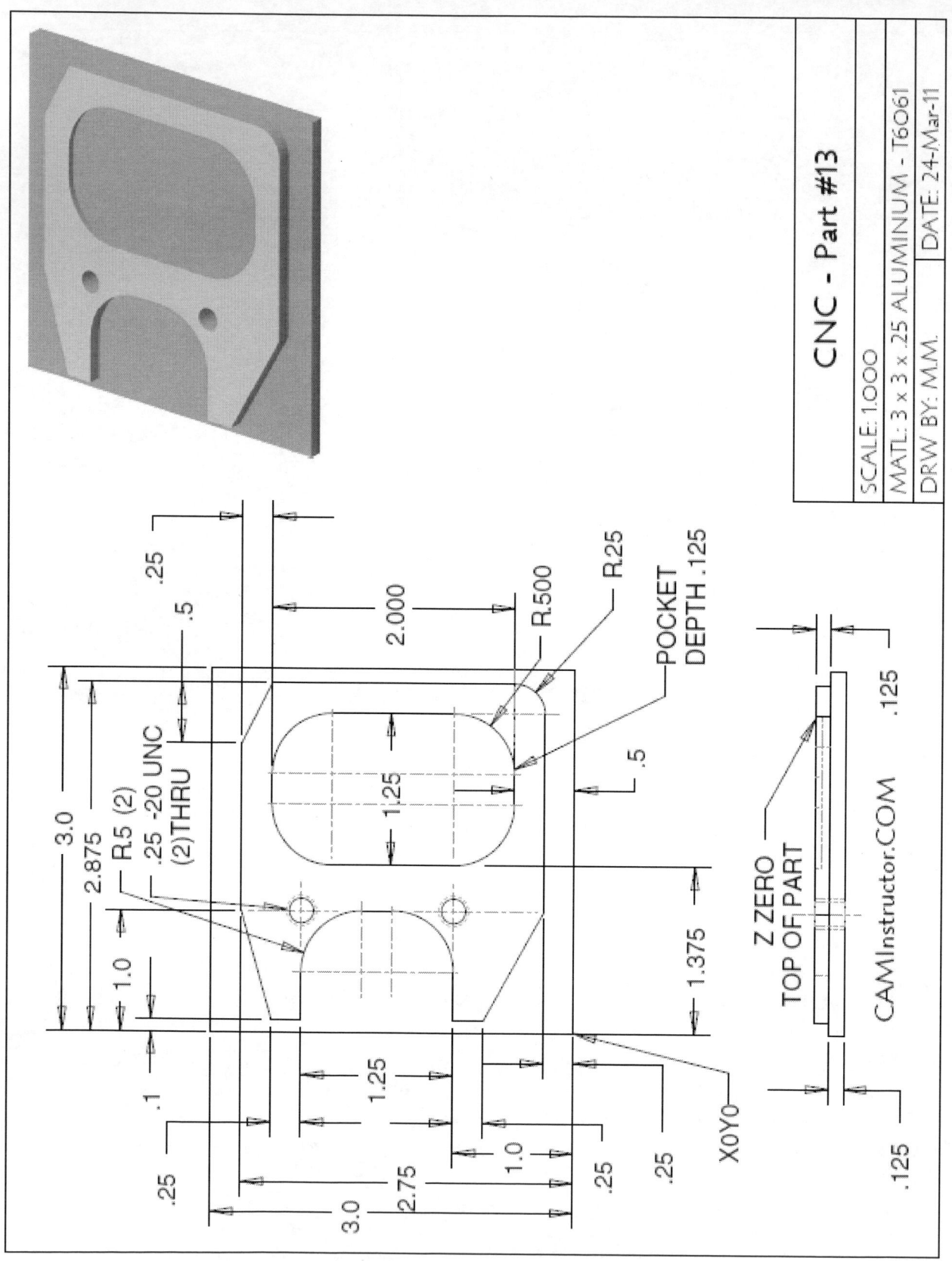

CNC - Part #13

SCALE: 1.000
MATL: 3 x 3 x .25 ALUMINUM - T6O61
DRW BY: M.M.   DATE: 24-Mar-11

POCKET DEPTH .125

R25

R.500

2.000

1.25

.5

.25

.5

3.0

2.875

R5 (2)

.25 -20 UNC
(2)THRU

1.0

.1

.25

1.25

2.75

3.0

1.0

.25

.25

1.375

Z ZERO
TOP OF PART

CAMInstructor.COM

.125

.125

X0Y0

LESSON-10 - CNC - PART #13

- **The Machining Process**
- **Ø.750" Endmill - Tool # 6**
  - Machine the profile and pocket using cutter compensation
  - 0.750" diameter end mill Spindle Speed = 2100 Feed rate = 25 IPM
- **Ø.375" Spot Drill - Tool # 7**
  - Spot Drill Spindle Speed = 2750 Feed rate = 11 IPM
- **Ø.201" Drill - Tool # 8**
  - 0.201" diameter Drill Spindle Speed = 4500 Feed rate = 15 IPM
- **Ø.25"-20 UNC Tap - Tool # 9**
  - 0.250-20 UNC Tap Spindle Speed = 1000 Feed rate = 50 IPM

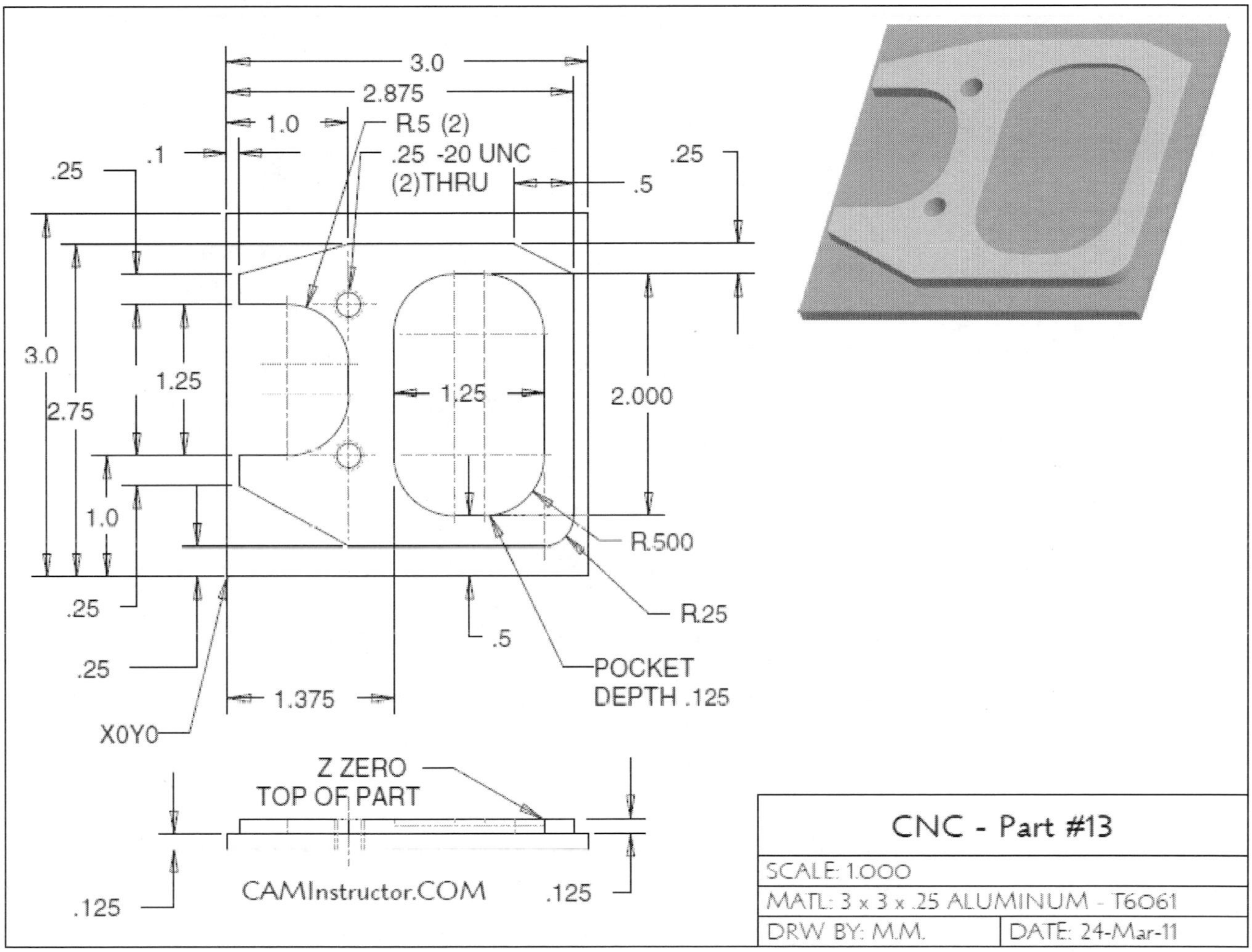

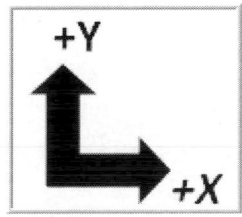

CNC - Part #13

SCALE: 1.000

MATL: 3 x 3 x .25 ALUMINUM - T6061

DRW BY: M.M.   DATE: 24-Mar-11

- ***WORK OUT THE ABSOLUTE X AND Y COORDINATES FOR THE VARIOUS POSITIONS TO MACHINE THE PART***
  - X0Y0 is at the lower left corner of the part

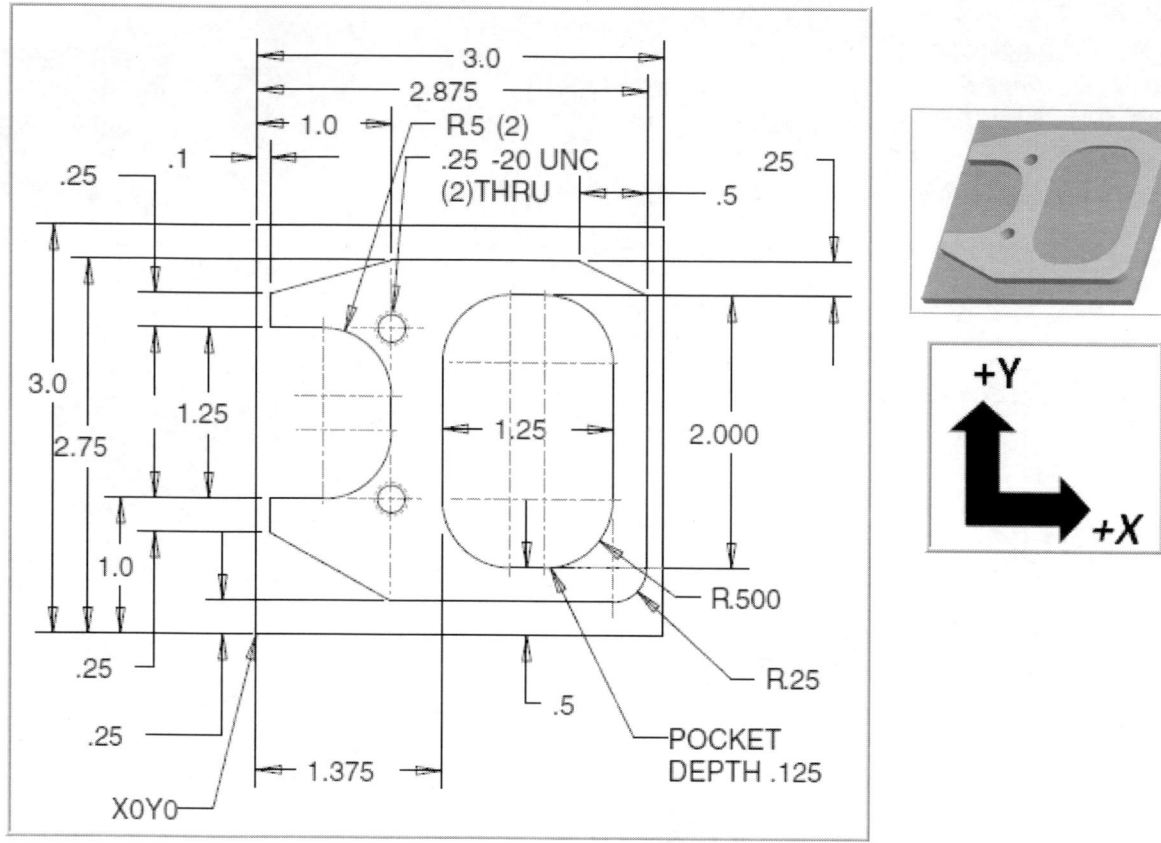

- ***WORK OUT THE ABSOLUTE X AND Y COORDINATES FOR THE TWO HOLES***

G90	X	Y
1		
2		

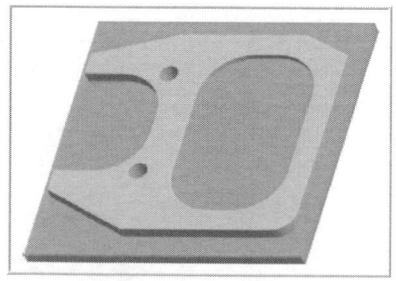

- **WORK OUT THE ABSOLUTE X AND Y COORDINATES FOR THE VARIOUS POSITIONS TO MACHINE THE PART - CONTOUR**
  - XOYO is at the lower left of the part

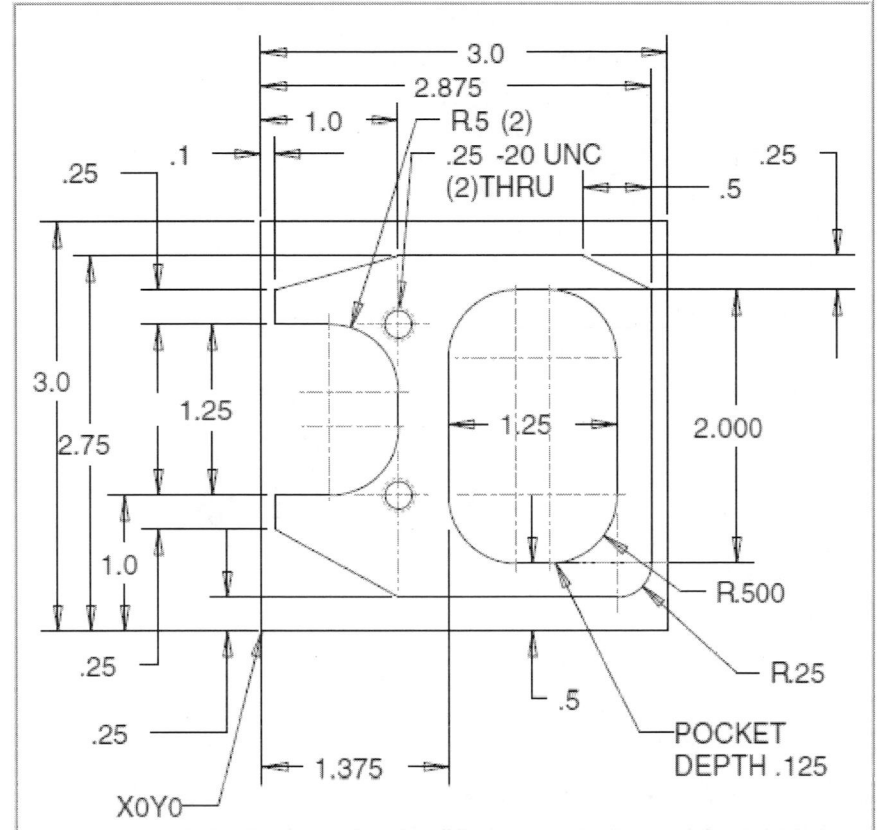

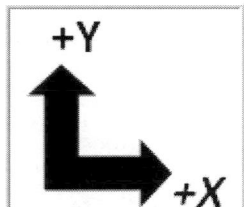

- **WORK OUT THE ABSOLUTE X AND Y COORDINATES FOR THE VARIOUS POSITIONS OF THE 0.75' DIAMETER END MILL TO MACHINE THE CONTOUR**

G90	X	Y	G90	X	Y
1			12		
2			13		
3			14		
4			15		
5			16		
6			17		
7					
8					
9					
10					
11					

- **WORK OUT THE ABSOLUTE X AND Y COORDINATES FOR THE VARIOUS POSITIONS TO MACHINE THE PART - POCKET**
  - X0Y0 is at the lower left of the part

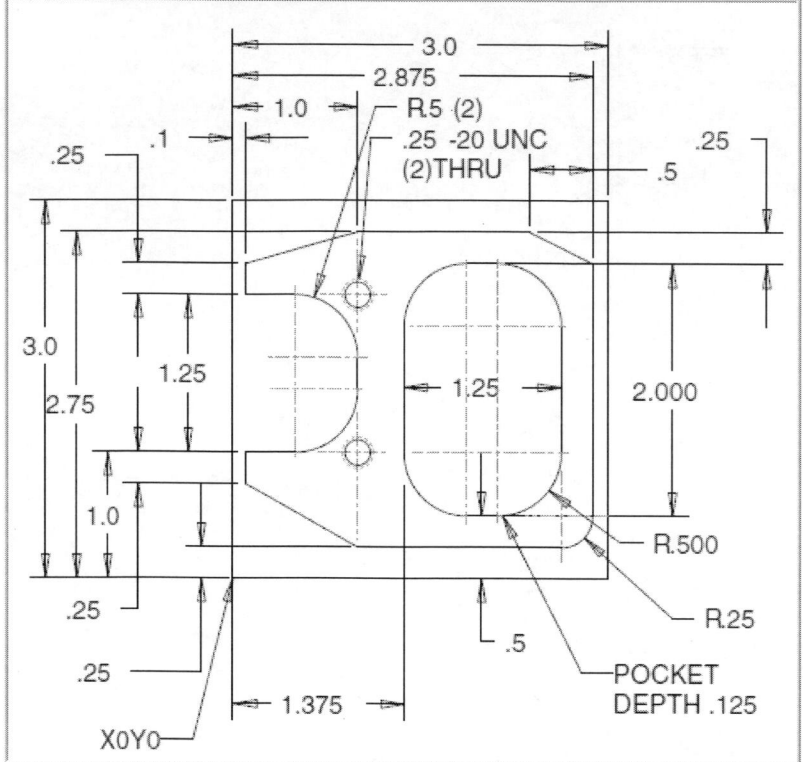

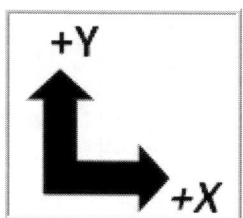

- **WORK OUT THE ABSOLUTE X AND Y COORDINATES FOR THE VARIOUS POSITIONS OF THE 0.75' DIAMETER END MILL TO MACHINE THE POCKET**

G90	X	Y
1		
2		
3		
4		
5		
6		
7		
8		
9		
10		
11		
12		
13		

- **CREATE THE PROGRAM TO MACHINE THE PART**
- **The Machining Process**
- **Ø.750" Endmill - Tool # 6**
    - Machine the profile and pocket using cutter compensation
    - 0.750" diameter end mill Spindle Speed = 2100 Feed rate = 25

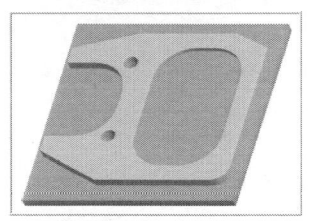

IPM

- **Ø.375" Spot Drill - Tool # 7**
    - Spot Drill Spindle Speed = 2750 Feed rate = 11 IPM
- **Ø.201" Drill - Tool # 8**
    - 0.201" diameter Drill Spindle Speed = 4500 Feed rate = 15 IPM
- **Ø.25"-20 UNC Tap - Tool # 9**
    - 0.201" diameter Drill Spindle Speed = 1000 Feed rate = 50 IPM

%
O888
N10   G20
N20   G00 G17 G40 G49 G80 G90 (MACHINE DEFAULT SETTING)
N30

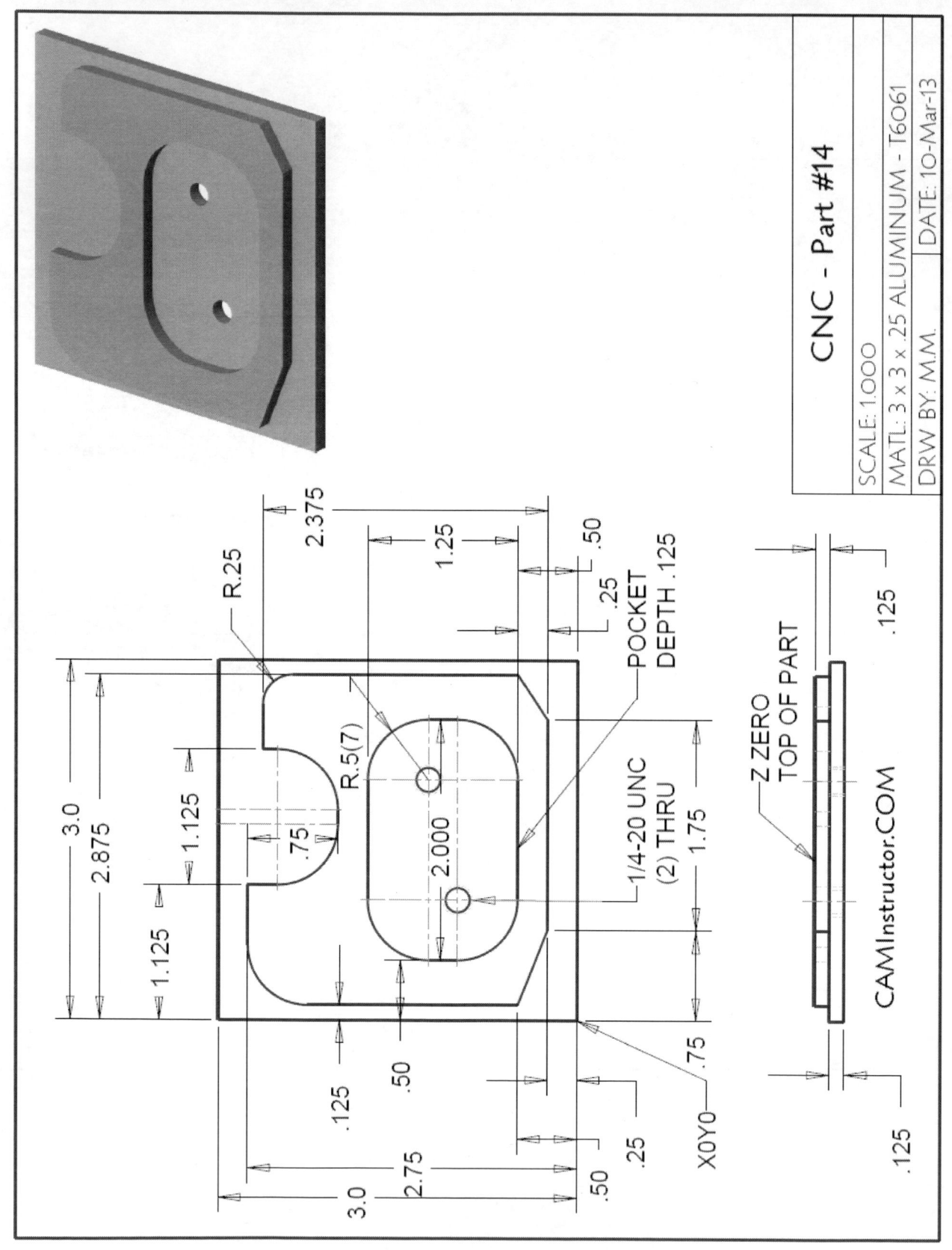

CNC - Part #14

SCALE: 1.000
MATL: 3 x 3 x .25 ALUMINUM - T6061
DRW BY: MM.   DATE: 10-Mar-13

R.25

2.375

1.25

.50

.25

POCKET
DEPTH .125

R.5(7)

3.0

2.875

1.125

.75

2.000

1/4-20 UNC
(2) THRU

1.75

1.125

.125

.50

2.75

3.0

.25

.50

X0Y0

.75

Z ZERO
TOP OF PART

.125

.125

CAMInstructor.COM

- **The Machining Process**
- **Ø.750" Endmill - Tool # 6**
  - Machine the profile and pocket using cutter compensation
  - 0.750" diameter end mill Spindle Speed = 2100 Feed rate = 25 IPM
- **Ø.375" Spot Drill - Tool # 7**
  - Spot Drill Spindle Speed = 2750 Feed rate = 11 IPM
- **Ø.201" Drill - Tool # 8**
  - 0.201" diameter Drill Spindle Speed = 4500 Feed rate = 15 IPM
- **Ø.25"-20 UNC Tap - Tool # 9**
  - 0.201" diameter Drill Spindle Speed = 1000 Feed rate = 50 IPM

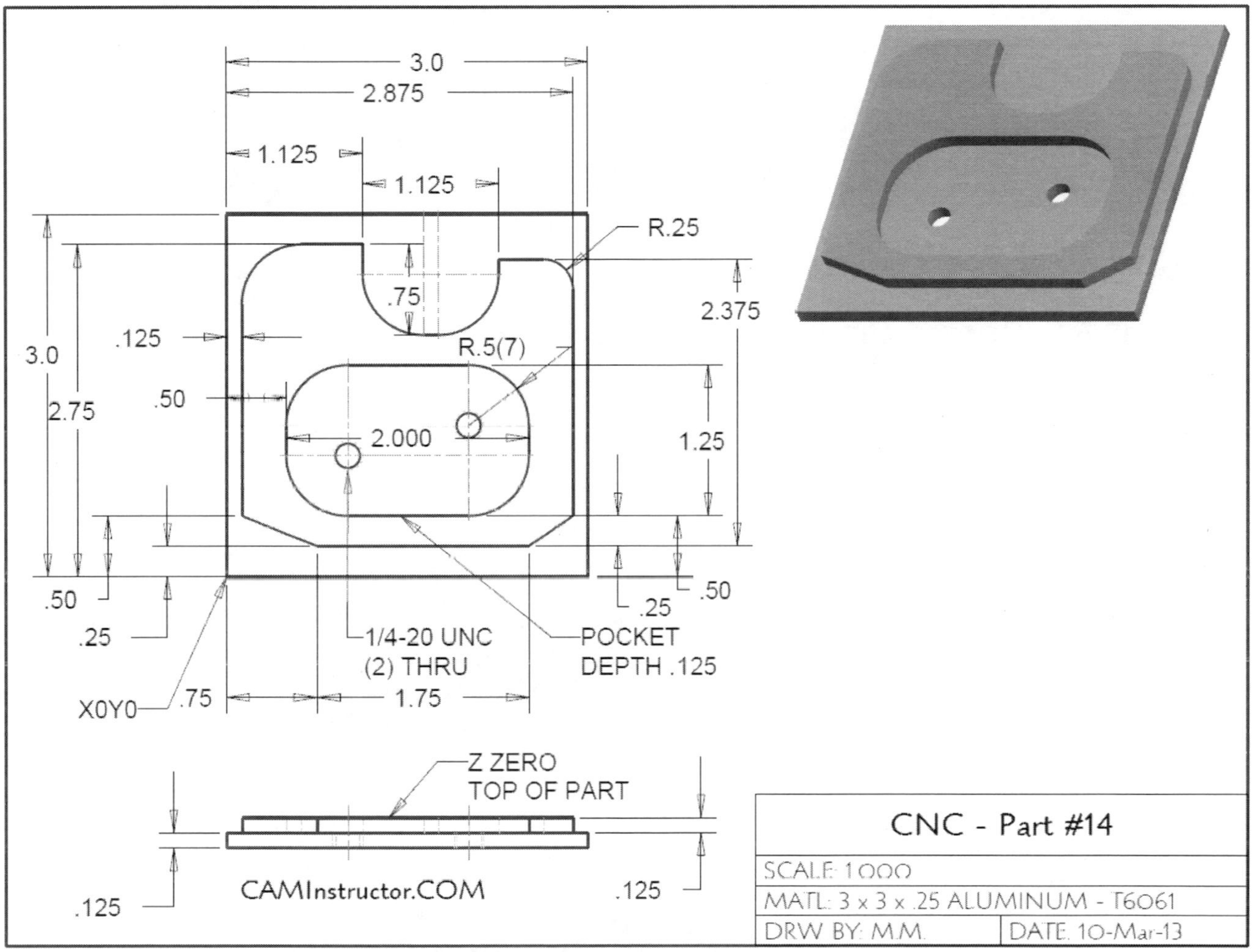

3.0	
2.875	
1.125	
1.125	
R.25	
.75	2.375
.125	R.5(7)
3.0	
2.75	1.25
.50	
2.000	
.50	.50
.25	.25
1/4-20 UNC (2) THRU	POCKET DEPTH .125
X0Y0 .75	1.75

Z ZERO
TOP OF PART

CAMInstructor.COM

.125 .125

CNC - Part #14

SCALE: 1.000
MATL: 3 x 3 x .25 ALUMINUM - T6061
DRW BY: M.M. DATE: 10-Mar-13

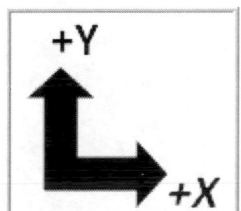

- **WORK OUT THE ABSOLUTE X AND Y COORDINATES FOR THE VARIOUS POSITIONS TO MACHINE THE PART**
  - X0Y0 is at the lower left of the part

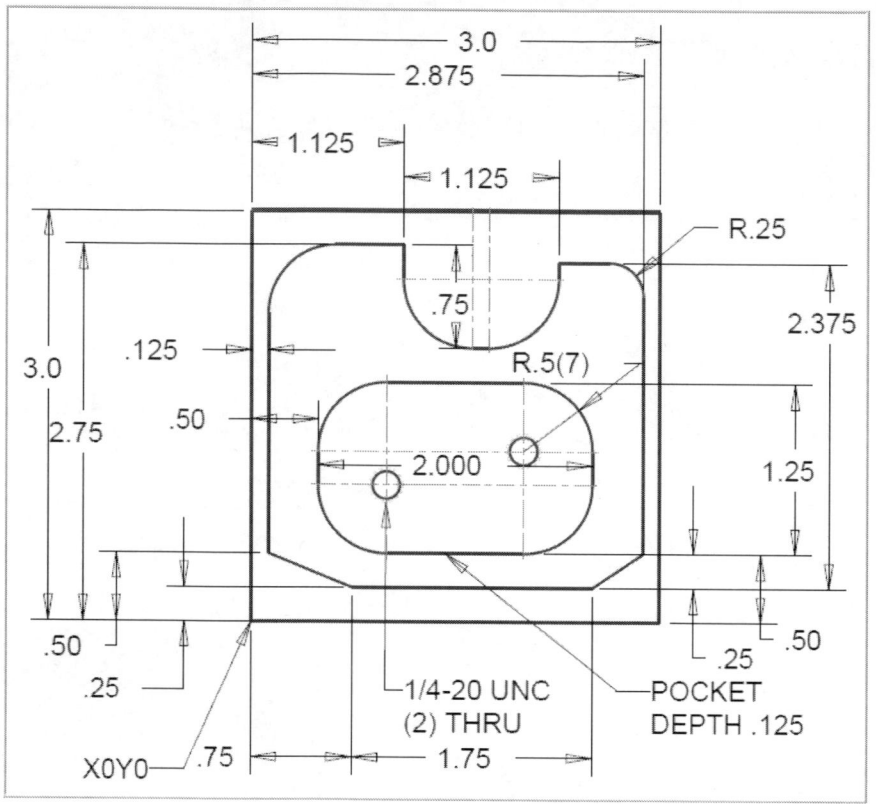

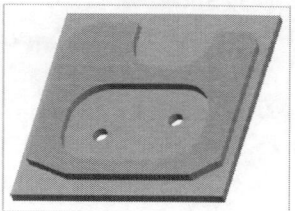

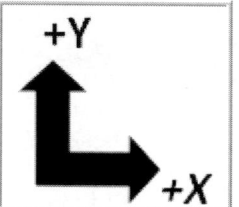

- **WORK OUT THE ABSOLUTE X AND Y COORDINATES FOR THE TWO HOLES**

G90	X	Y
1		
2		

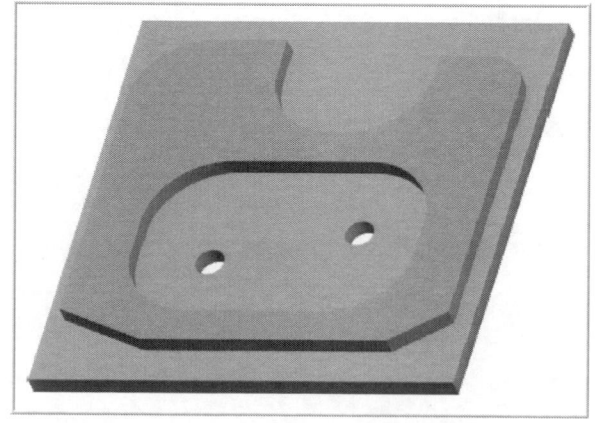

- **WORK OUT THE ABSOLUTE X AND Y COORDINATES FOR THE VARIOUS POSITIONS TO MACHINE THE PART - CONTOUR**
    - X0Y0 is at the lower left of the part

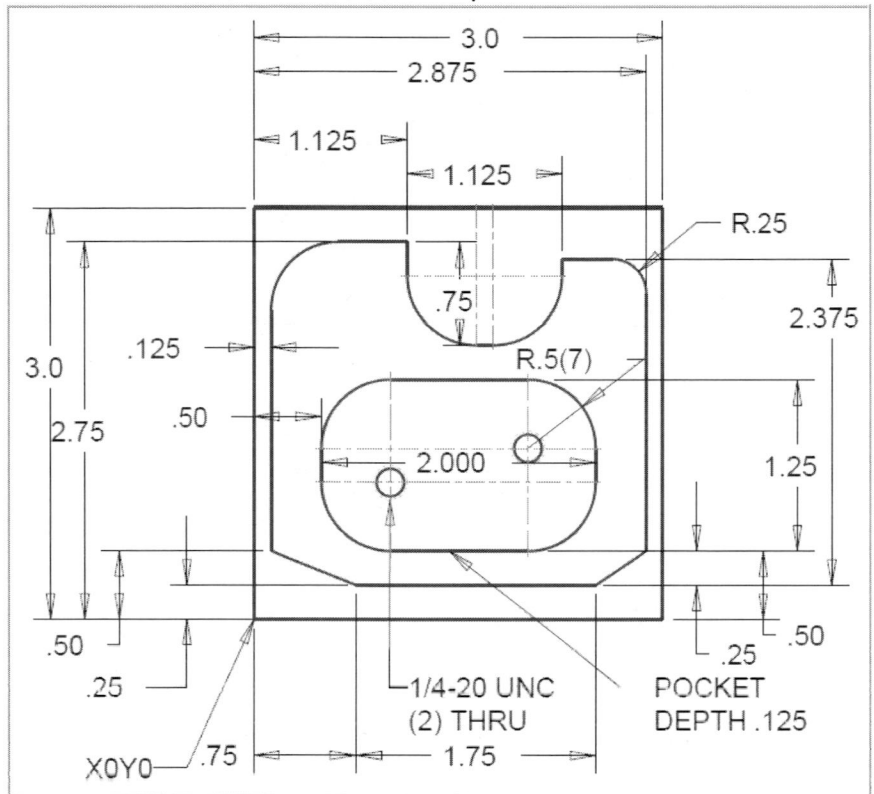

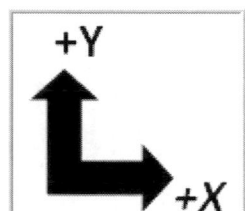

- **WORK OUT THE ABSOLUTE X AND Y COORDINATES FOR THE VARIOUS POSITIONS OF THE 0.75' DIAMETER END MILL TO MACHINE CONTOUR**

G90	X	Y	G90	X	Y
1			12		
2			13		
3			14		
4			15		
5			16		
6			17		
7					
8					
9					
10					
11					

- **WORK OUT THE ABSOLUTE X AND Y COORDINATES FOR THE VARIOUS POSITIONS TO MACHINE THE PART - POCKET**
  - X0Y0 is at the lower left of the part

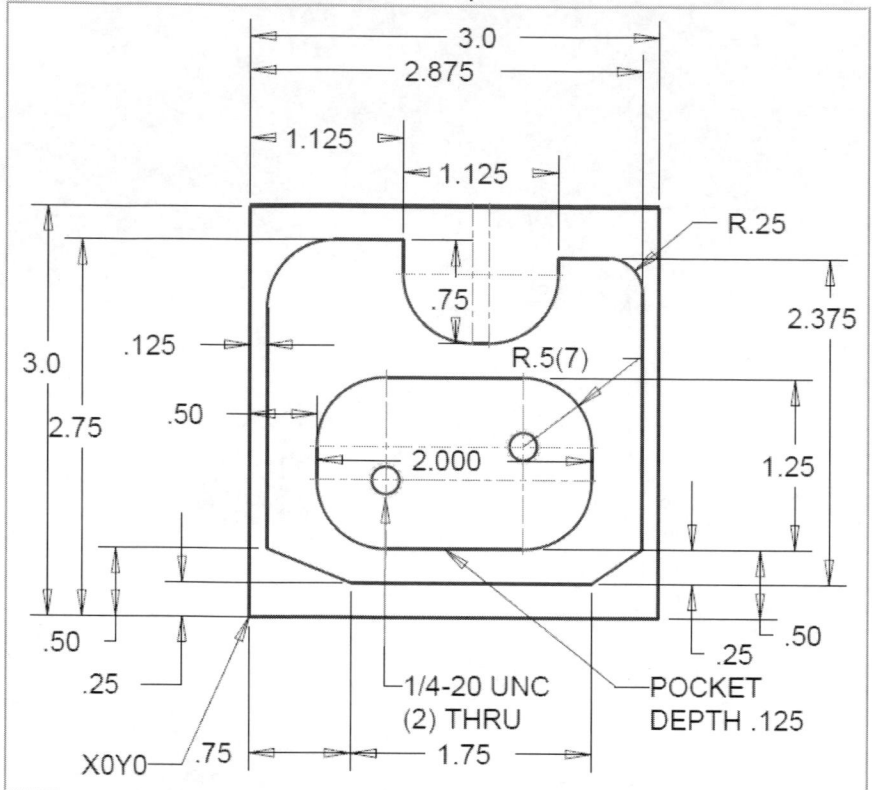

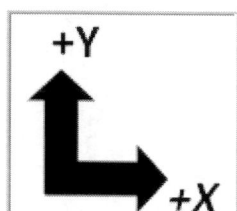

- **WORK OUT THE ABSOLUTE X AND Y COORDINATES FOR THE VARIOUS POSITIONS OF THE 0.75' DIAMETER END MILL TO MACHINE POCKET**

G90	X	Y
1		
2		
3		
4		
5		
6		
7		
8		
9		
10		
11		
12		
13		

- **CREATE THE PROGRAM TO MACHINE THE PART**
- **The Machining Process**
- **Ø.750" Endmill - Tool # 6**
  - Machine the profile and pocket using cutter compensation
  - 0.750" diameter end mill Spindle Speed = 2100 Feed rate = 25 IPM
- **Ø.375" Spot Drill - Tool # 7**
  - Spot Drill Spindle Speed = 2750 Feed rate = 11 IPM
- **Ø.201" Drill - Tool # 8**
  - 0.201" diameter Drill Spindle Speed = 4500 Feed rate = 15 IPM
- **Ø.25"-20 UNC Tap - Tool # 9**
  - 0.201" diameter Drill Spindle Speed = 1000 Feed rate = 50 IPM

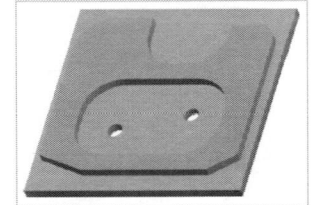

%
O003
N10   G20
N20   G00 G17 G40 G49 G80 G90 (MACHINE DEFAULT SETTING)
N30

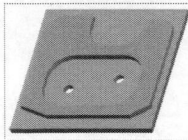

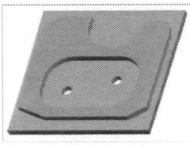

CNC PROGRAMMING
WORKBOOK - MILL

APPENDIX

camInstructor

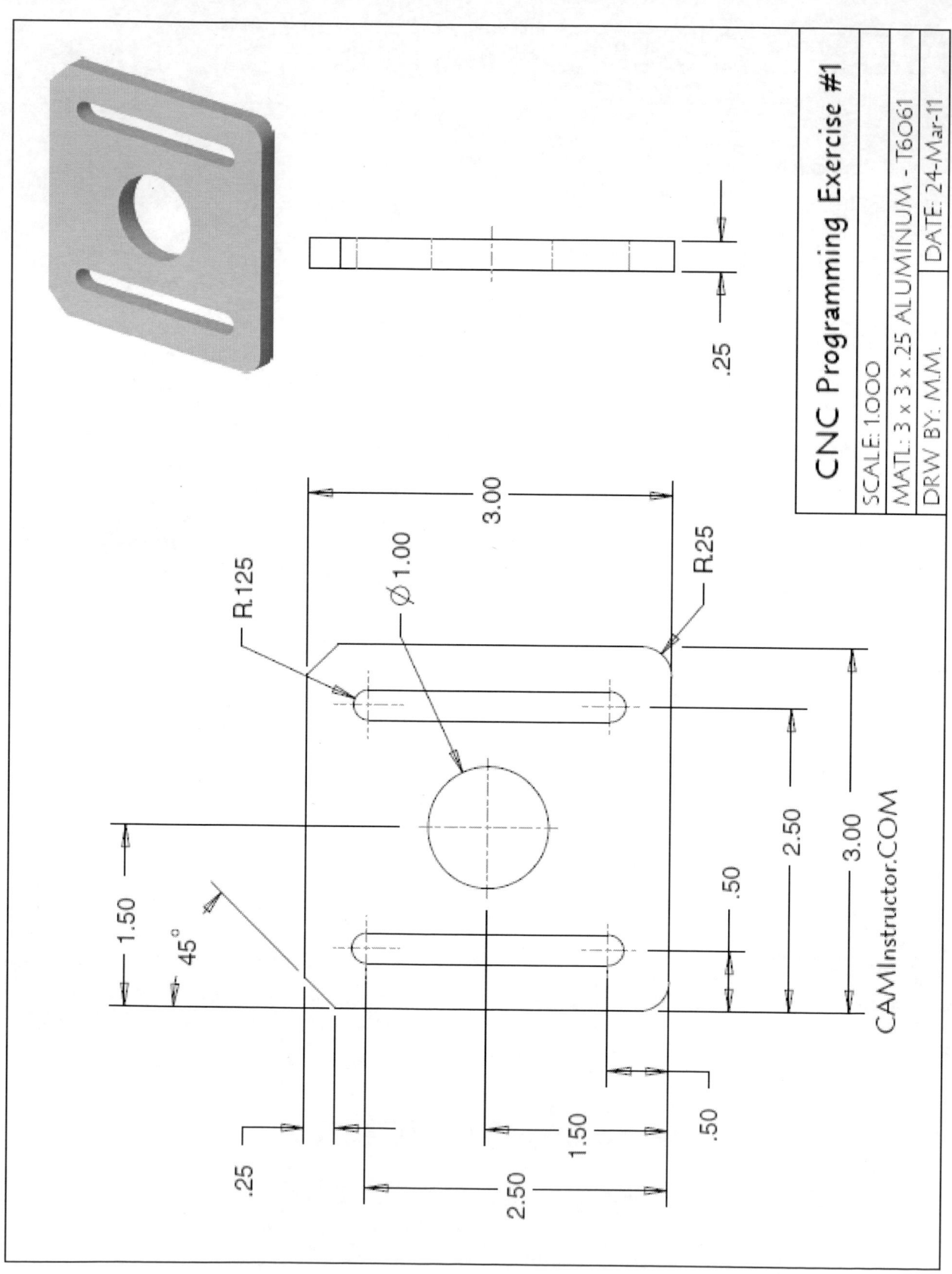

CNC Programming Exercise #1

SCALE: 1.000

MATL: 3 x 3 x .25 ALUMINUM - T6061

DRW BY: MM.

DATE: 24-Mar-11

R.125

Ø 1.00

R.25

3.00

1.50

45°

.50

2.50

3.00

.25

2.50

1.50

.50

CAMInstructor.COM

.25

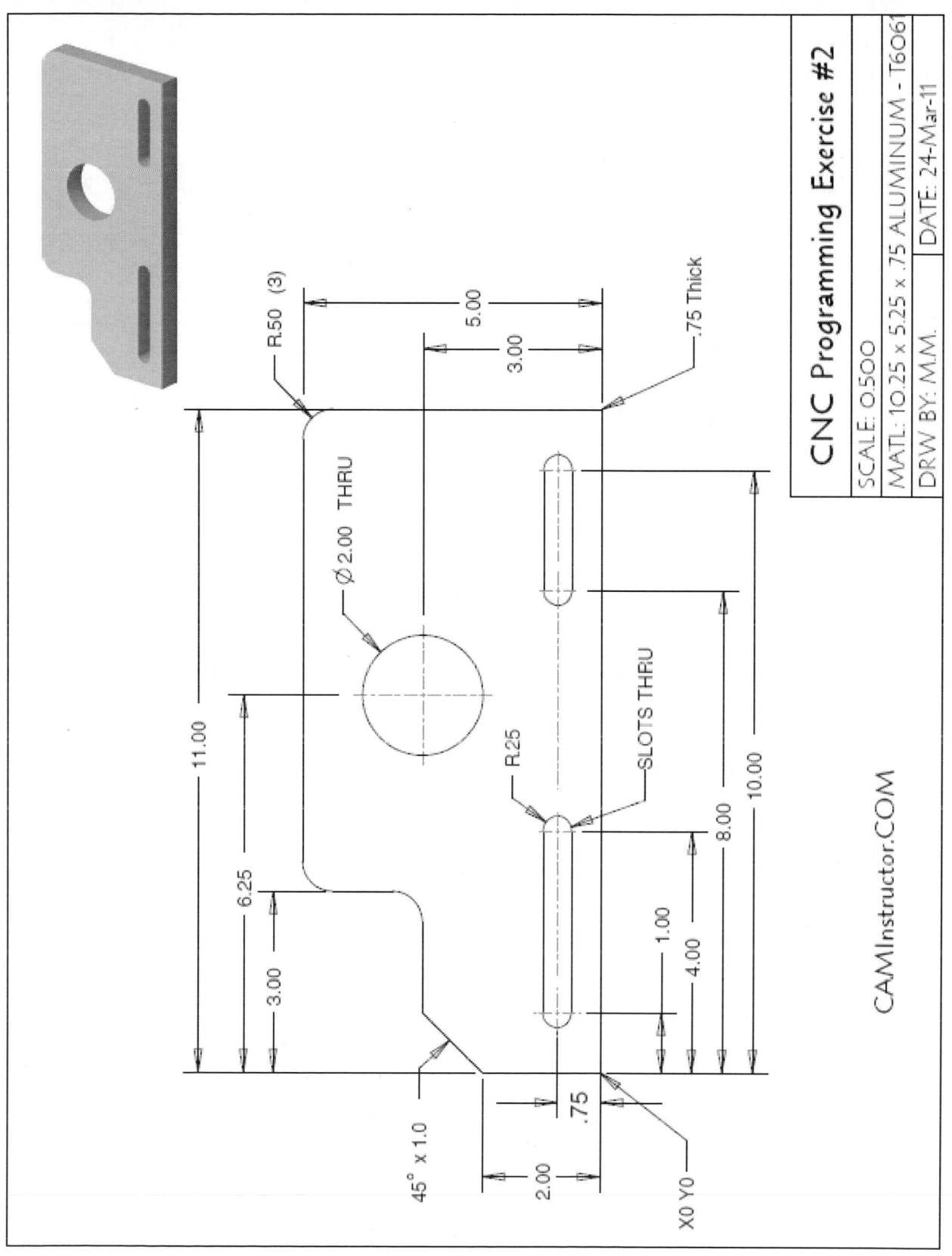

CNC Programming Exercise #2

SCALE: 0.500

MATL: 10.25 x 5.25 x .75 ALUMINUM - T6061

DRW BY: M.M.   DATE: 24-Mar-11

R.50 (3)

5.00

3.00

.75 Thick

Ø2.00 THRU

SLOTS THRU

R.25

11.00

6.25

3.00

10.00

8.00

1.00

4.00

45° x 1.0

.75

2.00

X0 Y0

CAMInstructor.COM

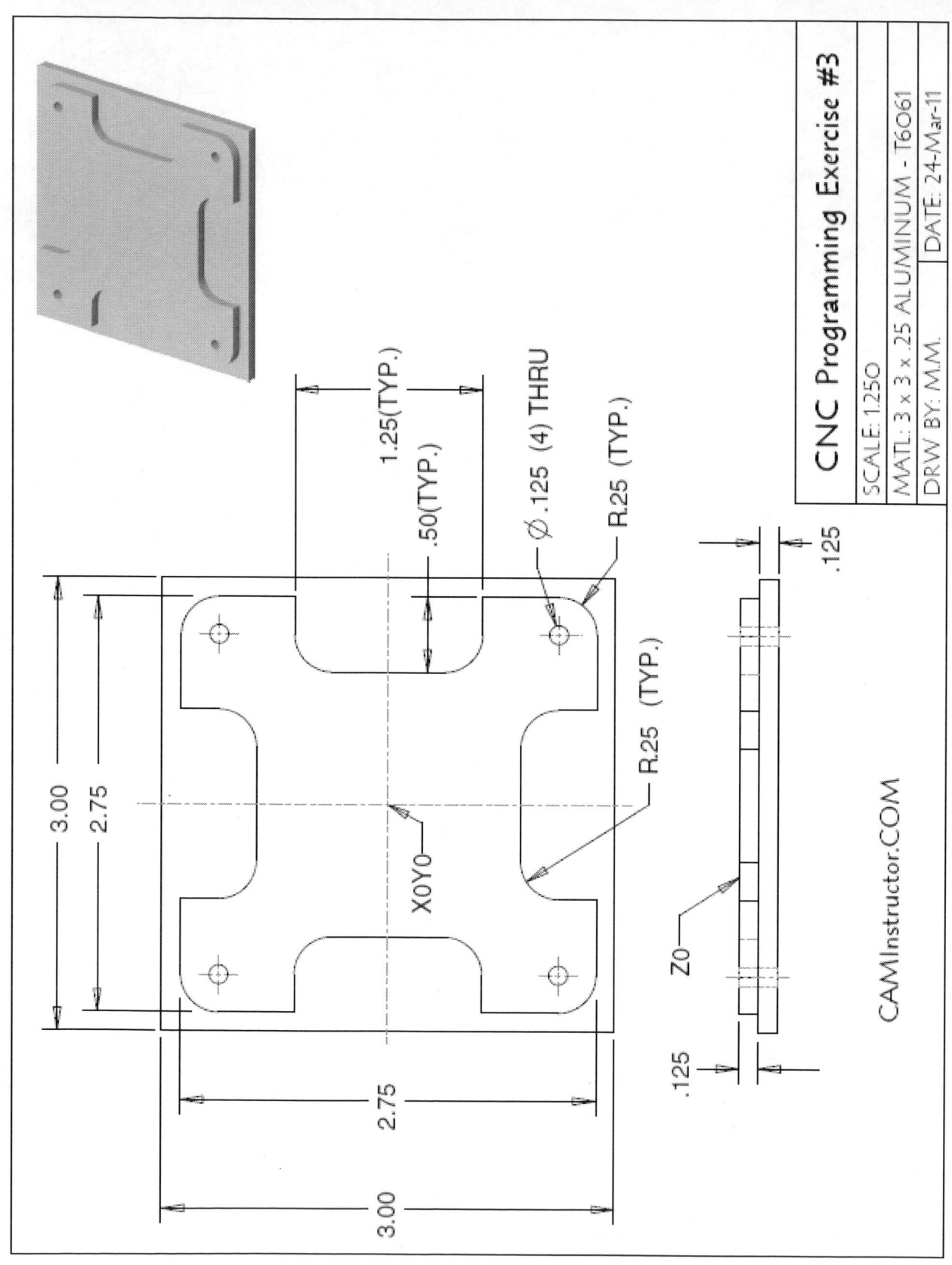

CNC Programming Exercise #3

SCALE: 1.250
MATL: 3 x 3 x .25 ALUMINUM - T6061
DRW BY: M.M.   DATE: 24-Mar-11

1.25(TYP.)
.50(TYP.)
Ø .125 (4) THRU
R.25 (TYP.)
R.25 (TYP.)
3.00
2.75
X0Y0
2.75
3.00
.125
.125
Z0

CAMInstructor.COM

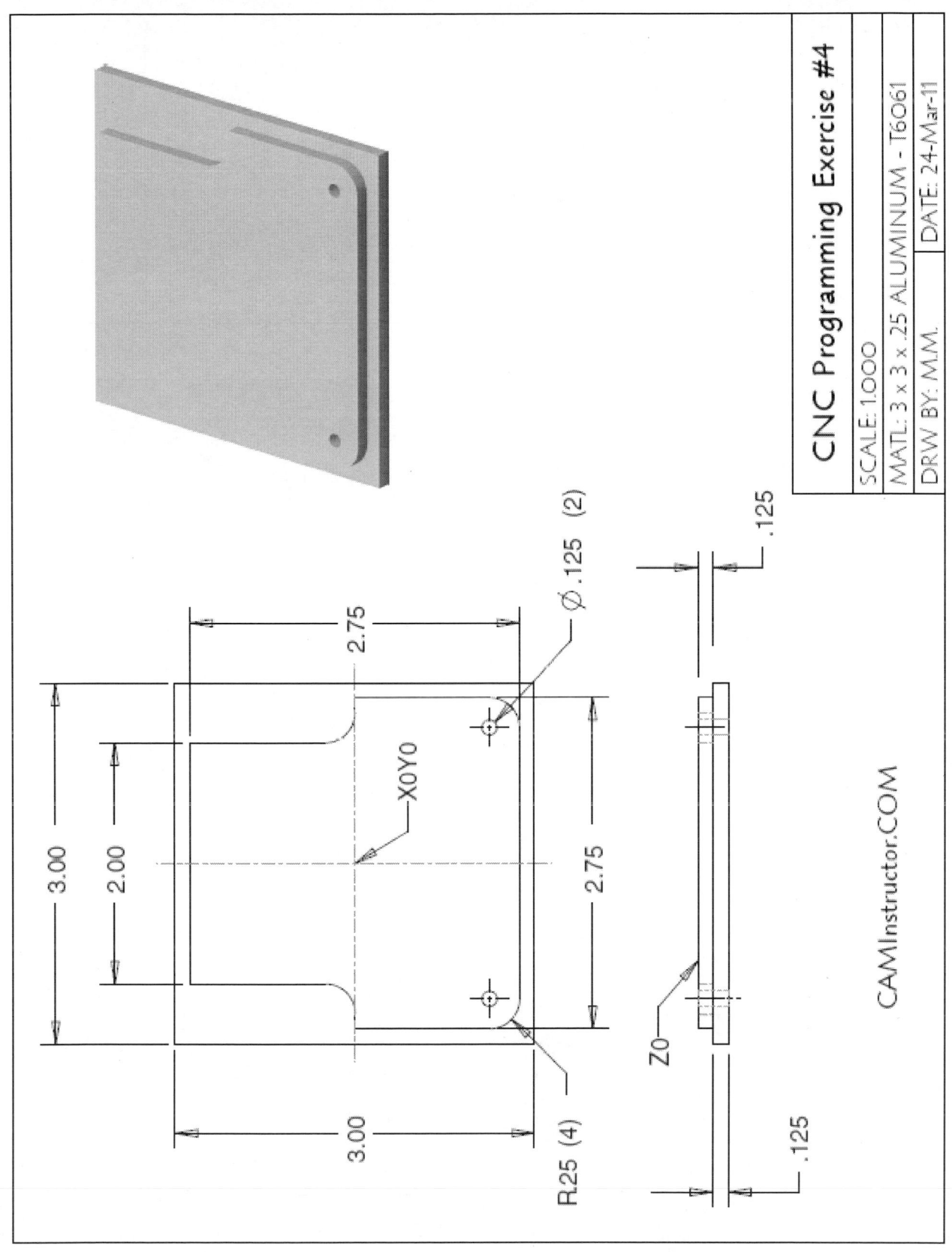

CNC Programming Exercise #4

SCALE: 1.000
MATL: 3 x 3 x .25 ALUMINUM - T6061
DRW BY: M.M.   DATE: 24-Mar-11

2.75

Ø .125 (2)

.125

3.00

2.00

X0Y0

2.75

Z0

R25 (4)

3.00

.125

CAMInstructor.COM

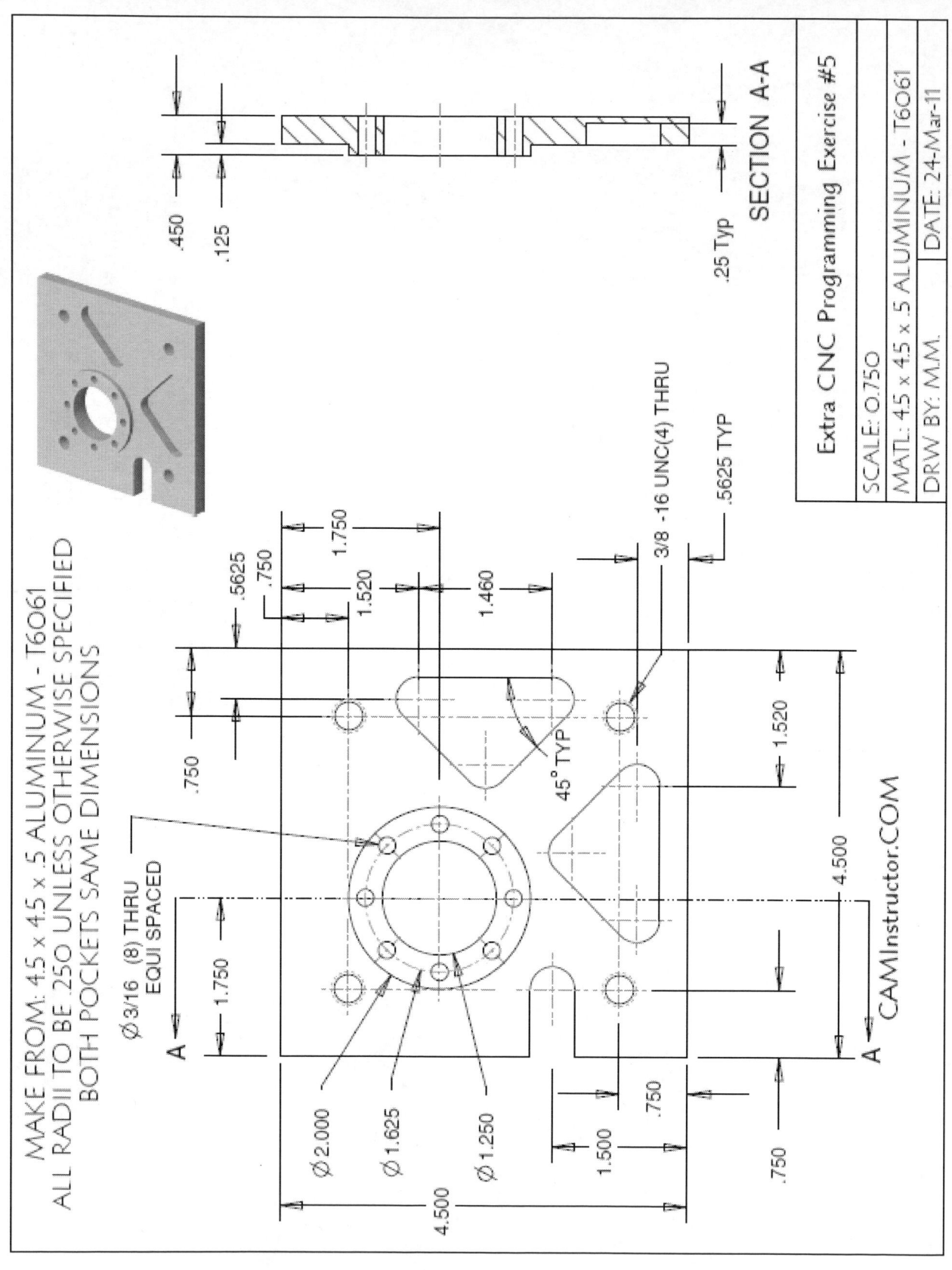

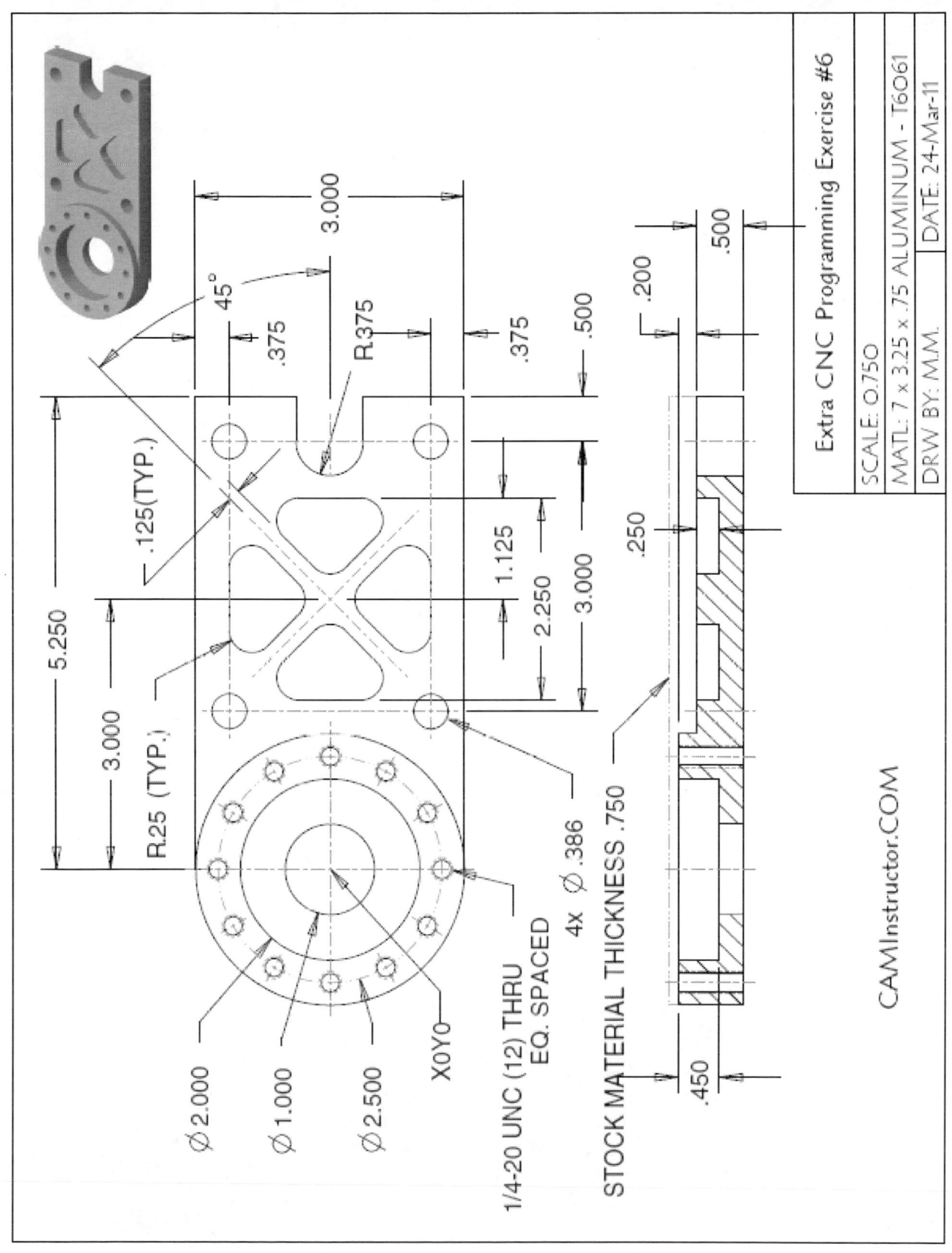

Instructions:

1. Create your own design.
2. The material size: 6" x 1.5" x .125" Aluminum
3. The part is held in the vise.
4. Locate the part flush with the left hand side of the vise jaw.
5. X0 Y0 is the top left hand corner of the material.
6. Z0 is the top of the material.
7. Center Drill is used as an engraving tool to machine the letters.
8. Spindle Speed: 5000 rpm
9. Feedrate: 12 in/min
10. Depth of Cut : -0.025"
11. Center Drill 2 mounting holes using Canned Cycle
12. Depth of Cut: -0.25
13. Minimum of five letters
14. You can use the suggested letter shapes & size or create your own lettering design.

Suggested Lettering:

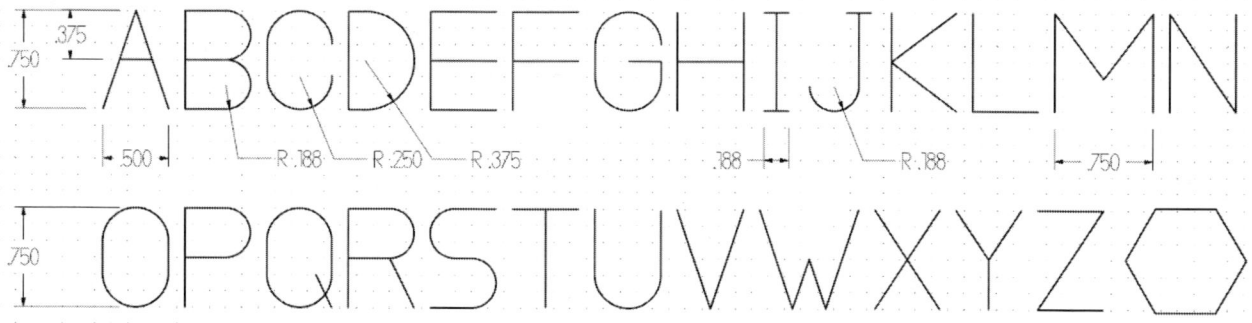

G00 RAPID POSITIONING MOTION
G01 LINEAR INTERPOLATION MOTION
G02 CIRCULAR INTERPOLATION MOTION - CLOCKWISE
G03 CIRCULAR INTERPOLATION MOTION - COUNTECLOCKWISE
G04 DWELL
G09 EXACT STOP
G10 PROGRAMMABLE OFFSET SETTING
G12 CW CIRCULAR POCKET MILLING
G13 CCW CIRCULAR POCKET MILLING
G17 CIRCULAR MOTION XY PLANE SELECTION (G02 or G03)
G18 CIRCULAR MOTION ZX PLANE SELECTION (G02 or G03)
G19 CIRCULAR MOTION YZ PLANE SELECTION (G02 or G03)
G20 VERIFY INCH COORDINATE POSITIONING
G21 VERIFY METRIC COORDINATE POSITIONING
G28 MACHINE ZERIO RETURN THRU REF. POINT
G29 MOVE TO LOCATION THROUGH G28 REF. POINT
G31 FEED UNTIL SKIP FUNCTION
G35 AUTOMATIC TOOL DIAMETER MEASUREMENT
G36 AUTOMATIC WORK OFFSET MEASUREMENT
G37 AUTOMATIC TOOL LENGTH MEASUREMENT
G40 CUTTER COMPENSATION CANCEL G41/G42/G141
G41 2D CUTTER COMPENSATION, LEFT (X, Y, D)
G42 2D CUTTER COMPENSATION, RIGHT (X, Y, D)
G43 TOOL LENGTH COMPESATION POSITIVE (H, Z)
G44 TOOL LENGTH COMPENATION NEGATIVE (H, Z)

G47 TEXT ENGRAVING (X, Y, Z, R, I, J, P, E, F)
G49 TOOL LENGTH COMPENSATION CANCEL G43/G44/G143)
G50 SCALING G51 CANCEL
G51 SCALING (X, Y, Z, P)
G52 WORK OFFSET COORDINATE POSITING
G52 GLOBAL WORK COORDINATE OFFSET SHIFT
G52 GLOBAL WORK COORDINATE OFFSET SHIFT
G53 MACHINE COORDAINTE POSITIONING, NON-MODAL (X, Y, Z, A, B)
G54 WORK OFSET COORDIANTE POSITIONING #1
G55 WORK OFSET COORDIANTE POSITIONING #2
G56 WORK OFSET COORDIANTE POSITIONING #3
G57 WORK OFSET COORDIANTE POSITIONING #4
G58 WORK OFSET COORDIANTE POSITIONING #5
G59 WORK OFSET COORDIANTE POSITIONING #6
G60 UNI-DIRECTIONAL POSITIONING (X, Y, Z, A, B)
G61 EXACT STOP, MODAL (X, Y, Z, A, B)
G64 EXACT STOP G61 MODE CANCEL
G65 MACRO SUB-ROUTINE CALL
G68 ROATION (G17, G18, G19, X, Y, Z, R)
G69 ROTATION G68 CANCEL
G70 BOLT HOLE CIRCLE with a CANNED CYCLE (I, J, L)

G71 BOLTHOLEARC with a CANNED CYCLE (I, J, K, L)
G72 BOLT HOLES ALONG AN ANGLE with a CANNED CYCLE (I, J, L)
G73 HIGH SPEED PECK DRILL CANNED CYCLE (X, Y, A, B, Z, I, J, K, Q, P, R, L, F)
G74 REVERSE TAPPING CANNED CYCLE (X, Y, A, B, Z, J, R, L, F)
G76 FINE BORING CANNED CYCLE (X, Y, A, B, Z, I, J, P, Q, R, L, F)
G77 BACK BORE CANNED CYCLE (X, Y, A, B, Z, I, J, Q, R, L, F)
G80 CANCEL CANNED CYCLE
G81 DRILL CANNED CYCLE (X, Y, A, B, Z, R, L, F)
G82 SPOT DRILL/COUNTERBORE CANNED CYCLE (X, Y, A, B, Z, P, R, L, F)
G83 PECK DRILL CANNED CYCLE (X, Y, A, B, Z, I, J, K, Q, P, R, L, F)
G84 TAPPING CANNED CYCLE (X, Y, A, B, Z, J, R, L, F)
G85 BORE IN, BORE OUT CANNED CYCLE (X, Y, A, B, Z, R, L, F)
G86 BORE IN, STOP, RAPID OUT CANNED CYCLE (X, Y, A, B, Z, R, L, F)
G87 BORE IN AND MANUAL RETRACT CANNED CYCLE (X, Y, A, B, Z, R, L, F)
G88 BORE IN, DWELL, MANUAL RETRACT CANNED CYCLE (X, Y, A, B, Z, P, R, L, F)
G89 BORE IN, DWELL, BORE OUT (X, Y, A, B, Z, P, R, L, F)
G90 ABSOLUTE POSITIONING
G91 INCREMENTAL POSITIONING
G92 GLOBAL WORK COORDINATE SYSTEM SHIFT (FANUC) (HAAS)
G92 SET WORK COORDINATE VALUE (YA SNAC)
G93 INVERSE TIME FEED MODE ON
G94 INVERSE TIME FEED MODE OFF/FEED PER MINUTE ON
G98 CANNED CYCLE INITIAL POINT RETURN
G99 CANNED CYCLE "R" PLANE RETURN

M00 PROGRAM STOP
M01 OPTIONAL PROGRAM STOP
M02 PROGRAM END
M03 SPINDLE ON CLOCKWISE
M04 SPINDLE ON COUTERCLOCKWISE
M05 SPINDLE STOP
M06 TOOL CHANGE
M08 COOLANT ON
M09 COOLANT OFF
M19 ORIENT SPINDLE (P, R)
M21-M28 OPTIONAL USER M CODE INTERFACE WITH M-FIN SIGNAL
M30 PROGRAM END AN RESET
M31 CHIP AUGER FORWARD
M32 CHIP AUGER REVERSE
M33 CHIP AUGER STOP
M34 COOLANT SPIGOT POSITION DOWN, INCREMENT
M35 COOLANT SPIGOT POSITION UP, DECREMENT
M36 PALET PART READY
M39 ROTATE TOOL TURRET
M41 SPINDLE LOW GEAR OVERRIDE
M42 SPINDLE HIGH GEAR OVERRIDE
M50 EXECUTE PALLET CHANGE

M51-M58 OPTIONAL USER M CODE SET
M59 OUTPUT RELAY SET (N)
M61-M68 OPTIONAL USER M CODE CLEAR
M69 OUTPUT RELAY CLEAR (N)
M75 SET G35 OR G136 REFERENCE POINT
M76 CONTROL DISPLAY INACTIVE
M77 CONTROL DISPLAY ACTIVE
M78 ALARM IF SKIP SIGNAL FOUND
M79 ALARM IF SKIP SIGNAL NOT FOUND
M80 AUTOMATIC DOOR OPEN
M81 AUTOMATIC DOOR CLOSE
M82 TOOL UNCLAMP
M83 AUTO AIR JET ON
M84 AUTO AIR JET OFF
M86 TOOL CLAMP
M88 COOLANT THROUGH SPINDLE ON
M89 COOLANT THROUGH SPINDLE OFF
M93 AXIS POS CAPTURE START (P, Q)
M94 AXIS POS CAPTURE STOP
M95 SLEEP MODE
M96 JUMP IF NO SIGNAL (P, Q)
M97 LOCAL SUB-PROGRAM CALL (P, L)
M98 SUB-PROGRAM CALL (P, L)
M99 SUB-PROGRAM/ROUTINE RETURN OR LOOP
M109 INTERACTIVE USER INPUT (P)

Standard Drill Sizes - Inches

Drill Size	Decimal Equiv.	Drill Size	Decimal Equiv.	Drill Size	Decimal Equiv.	Drill Size	Decimal Equiv.
80 = .0135		43 = .089		8 = .199		25/64 = .3906	
79 = .0145		42 = .0935		7 = .201		X = .397	
1/64 = .0156		3/32 = .0938		13/64 = .2031		Y = .404	
78 = .016		41 = .096		6 = .204		13/32 = .4063	
77 = .018		40 = .098		5 = .2055		Z = .413	
76 = .020		39 = .0995		4 = .209		27/64 = .4219	
75 = .021		38 = .1015		3 = .213		7/16 = .4375	
74 = .0225		37 = .104		7/32 = .2188		29/64 = .4531	
73 = .024		36 = .1065		2 = .221		15/32 = .4688	
72 = .025		7/64 = .1094		1 = .228		31/64 = .4844	
71 = .026		35 = .110		A = .234		1/2 = .500	
70 = .028		34 = .111		15/64 = .2344		33/64 = .5156	
69 = .0292		33 = .113		B = .238		17/32 = .5313	
68 = .031		32 = .116		C = .242		35/64 = .5469	
1/32 = .0313		31 = .120		D = .246		9/16 = .5625	
67 = .032		1/8 = .1250		1/4 (E) = .250		37/64 = .5781	
66 = .033		30 = .1285		F = .257		19/32 = .5938	
65 = .035		29 = .136		G = .261		39/64 = .6094	
64 = .036		28 = .1405		17/64 = .2656		5/8 = .625	
63 = .037		9/64 = .1406		H = .266		41/64 = .6406	
62 = .038		27 = .144		I = .272		21/32 = .6563	
61 = .039		26 = .147		J = .277		43/64 = .6719	
60 = .040		25 = .1495		K = .281		11/16 = .6875	
59 = .041		24 = .152		9/32 = .2813		45/64 = .7031	
58 = .042		23 = .154		L = .290		23/32 = .7188	
57 = .043		5/32 = .1563		M = .295		47/64 = .7344	
56 = .0465		22 = .157		19/64 = .2969		3/4 = .750	
3/64 = .0469		21 = .159		N = .302		49/64 = .7656	
55 = .052		20 = .161		5/16 = .3125		25/32 = .7813	
54 = .055		19 = .166		O = .316		51/64 = .7969	
53 = .0595		18 = .1695		P = .323		13/16 = .8125	
1/16 = .0625		11/64 = .1719		21/64 = .3281		53/64 = .8281	
52 = .0635		17 = .173		Q = .332		27/32 = .8438	
51 = .067		16 = .177		R = .339		55/64 = .8594	
50 = .070		15 = .180		11/32 = .3438		7/8 = .875	
49 = .073		14 = .182		S = .348		57/64 = .8906	
48 = .076		13 = .185		T = .358		29/32 = .9063	
5/64 = .0781		3/16 = .1875		23/64 = .3594		59/64 = .9219	
47 = .0785		12 = .189		U = .368		15/16 = .9375	
46 = .081		11 = .191		3/8 = .375		61/64 = .9531	
45 = .082		10 = .1935		V = .377		31/32 = .9688	
44 = .086		9 = .196		W = .386		63/64 = .9844	

Inch Tap Drill Sizes

INCH SIZES - NATIONAL COARSE UNC			INCH SIZES - NATIONAL FINE UNF	
TAP SIZE	**DRILL SIZE**		**TAP SIZE**	**DRILL SIZE**
#1-64	#53		#0-80	3/64"
#2-56	#51		#1-72	#53
#3-48	5/64"		#2-64	#50
#4-40	#43		#3-56	#46
#5-40	#39		#4-48	#42
#6-32	#36		#5-44	#37
#8-32	#29		#6-40	#33
#10-24	#25		#8-36	#29
#12-24	#17		#10-32	#21
1/4-20	#7		#12-28	#15
5/16-18	F		1/4-28	#3
3/8-16	5/16		5/16-24	I
7/16-14	U		3/8-24	Q
1/2-13	27/64		7/16-20	W
9/16-12	31/64		1/2-20	29/64
5/8-11	17/32		9/16-18	33/64
3/4-10	21/32		5/8-18	37/64
7/8-9	49/64		3/4-16	11/16
1"-8	7/8		7/8-14	13/16
1-1/8-7	63/64		1"-14	15/16
1-1/4-7	1-7/64		1-1/8-12	1-3/64
1-1/2-6	1-11/32		1-1/4-12	1-11/64
1-3/4-5	1-35/64		1-1/2-12	1-27/64
2"-4-1/2	1-25/32		1-3/4-12	1-43/64
			2"-12	1-59/64

METRIC COARSE SIZES

TAP SIZE	DRILL SIZE
1mm x .25	.75mm
1.1 x .25	.85
1.2 x .25	.95
1.4 x .3	1.1
1.6 x .35	1.25
1.7 x .35	1.3
1.8 x .35	1.45
2 x .4	1.6
2.2 x .45	1.75
2.5 x .45	2.05
3 x .5	2.5
3.5 x .6	2.9
4 x .7	3.3
4.5 x .75	3.7
5 x .8	4.2
6 x 1	5
7 x 1	6
8 x 1.25	6.8
9 x 1.25	7.8
10 x 1.5	8.5
11 x 1.5	9.5
12 x 1.75	10.2
14 x 2	12
16 x 2	14
18 x 2.5	15.5
20 x 2.5	17.5
22 x 2.5	19.5
24 x 3	21
27 x 3	24
30 x 3.5	26.5

METRIC FINE SIZES

TAP SIZE	DRILL SIZE
4 mm x .35	3.6mm
4 x .5	3.5
5 x .5	4.5
6 x .5	5.5
6 x .75	5.25
7 x .75	6.25
8 x .5	7.5
8 x .75	7.25
8 x 1	7
9 x 1	8
10 x .75	9.25
10 x 1	9
10 x 1.25	8.8
11 x 1	10
12 x .75	11.25
12 x 1	11
12 x 1.5	10.5
14 x 1	13
14 x 1.25	12.8
14 x 1.5	12.5
16 x 1	15
16 x 1.5	14.5
18 x 1	17
18 x 2	16
20 x 1	19
20 x 1.5	18.5
20 x 2	18
22 x 1	21
22 x 1.5	20.5
22 x 2	20
24 x 1.5	22.5
24 x 2	22
26 x 1.5	24.5
27 x 1.5	25.5
27 x 2	25
28 x 1.5	26.5
30 x 1.5	28.5
30 x 2	28

CENTER DRILLING

Before most drilling operations take place a starting drill must be programmed to make a small hole for the larger drill that will follow. The tool used to make the starting hole is known as a center drill, sizes of center drills vary and the use of the different sizes is governed by the size of the drill that will be used after. The following is a chart that will assist in choosing the proper size of the center drill and programming the correct Z depth.

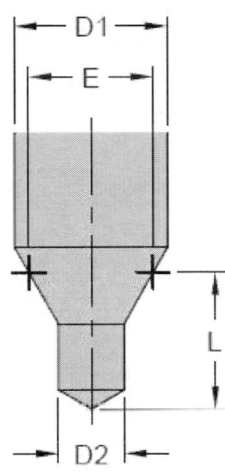

Number	D1	D2	E	L
# 1	0.125	0.047	0.100	0.106
# 2	0.188	0.078	0.150	0.163
# 3	0.250	0.110	0.200	0.219
# 4	0.312	0.125	0.250	0.269
# 5	0.438	0.188	0.350	0.382
# 6	0.500	0.218	0.400	0.438
# 7	0.625	0.250	0.500	0.538
# 8	0.750	0.312	0.600	0.651

DRILL POINT LENGTH

On most engineering drawings the finished depth of the hole will be given from the front edge of the part to the end of the parallel part of the hole (not including the drill point). This poses a programming problem because we program from the point of the drill so any Z depth we specify has to include the length of the drill point. To do this we have a calculation to perform based on the diameter of the drill and the angle of the drill point (usually 118°). Quite simply the calculation is as follows:

Drill Point Length = Diameter x Constant

Where DIA. refers to the drill diameter and the constant is stated in the following chart

DRILL ANGLE CONSTANTS			
60°=	0.866	110°=	0.350
75°=	0.652	118°=	0.300
80°=	0.596	120°=	0.289
82°=	0.575	135°=	0.207
90°=	0.500	150°=	0.134
100°=	0.420	180°=	0.000

Mill Appendix - 18